HISTORY OF THE PAPACY IN THE 19TH CENTURY

J. B. BURY

History of the Papacy in the 19th Century

LIBERTY AND AUTHORITY IN THE ROMAN CATHOLIC CHURCH

EDITED BY R. H. MURRAY

AUGMENTED EDITION

Vatican Council I · Vatican Council II

Introduction, epilogue and bibliographical notes by

Frederick C. Grant

SCHOCKEN BOOKS · NEW YORK

This edition is published by arrangement with Macmillan and Company, Ltd., London, under whose imprint *History of the Papacy in the Nineteenth Century* first appeared in 1930.

Library of Congress card catalog No. 64-22610
Manufactured in the United States of America

CONTENTS

THE POPES

1775	Pius VI (Braschi)
1800	Pius VII (Chiaramonti)
1823	Leo XII (Della Genga)
1829	Pius VIII (Castiglioni)
1831	Gregory XVI (Capellari)
1846	Pius IX (Mastai-Ferretti)
1878	Leo XIII (Pecci)
1903	Pius X (Sarto)
1914	Benedict XV (Della Chiesa)
1922	Pius XI (Ratti)
1939	Pius XII (Pacelli)
1958	John XXIII (Roncalli)
1963	Paul VI (Montini)

Abbreviations

Bettenson = Henry Bettenson, *Documents of the Christian Church,* 2d ed. Oxford 1963.

Denziger = Henricus Denziger, *Enchiridion Symbolorum, Definitionum et Declarationum de Rebus Fidei et Morum,* 32d ed. by Adolfus Schönmetzer, Herder 1963.

Heussi = Karl Heussi, *Kompendium der Kirchengeschichte,* 12th ed. Tübingen, Mohr 1960.

Mirbt = Carl Mirbt, *Quellen zur Geschichte des Papsttums und des Römischen Katholizismus,* 4th ed. Tübingen, Mohr 1924.

FOREWORD

Like many a classical work of art, like many an important historical work, ancient and modern, Bury's *History of the Papacy in the Nineteenth Century* is a torso, barely a third of its intended—or at least implied—length, and far short of the length suggested by its title. But this third, the central section, covers the most important years of the century. Whether the manuscript of the first third (1800–1864) or the final third, covering the long and important reign of Pope Leo XIII, was ever written, or the lectures ever delivered, we cannot ascertain. The present course was delivered in 1908. Bury's great work on *The Invasion of Europe by the Barbarians,* edited by F. J. C. Hearnshaw and published in 1928, was a series of fifteen lectures repeated from time to time during the years of his Regius Professorship at Cambridge (1902-27). This work was evidently complete. But the *History of the Papacy* fared differently; its multitudinous footnotes and references had to be checked by the editor, Canon Murray, and the periods before and after 1864-78 were left blank. But these fifteen years were most crucial for the Papacy and for the Church, and indeed for the whole of Europe in its relations with the Roman Catholic Church. Here a *third* of a loaf, not a half, is better than none!

The book was edited with a glowing and extended Memoir by the Rev. R. H. Murray of Pershore Abbey, and appeared in London in 1930.[1] In addition to a sketch of Bury's life and career from his boyhood in Ireland to his triumphant years as the chief of British historians, the Regius Professor of Modern History at Cambridge University, Canon Murray supplied a characterization of his historical point of view and method. This characterization applies to Bury's whole output of historical works, including the *History of the Papacy in the Nineteenth Century.* The same qualities are found in his Harvard Lectures on *The Ancient Greek Historians,* his classic *Life of St Patrick,* his *History of Greece* and *History of the Roman Empire,* his *Darwin and Modern Science,* his *History of Freedom of Thought, The Idea of Progress, A History of the Later Roman Empire from Arcadius to Irene,* and *A History of the Eastern Roman Empire from the Fall of Irene to the Accession of Basil I.* In his Inaugural Lecture at Cambridge (January 26, 1903),[2] Bury "declared the lofty doc-

[1] Robert Henry Murray, Canon of Worcester from 1933 to 1940, was educated at Queen's College, Belfast, and Trinity College, Dublin, and hence knew Professor Bury for many years—over thirty. In 1914–16 he was Chaplain to the Forces, and was in the Ministry of Information in 1914–18 and the Ministry of Food 1916–18. In 1922 he was expelled from Ireland by the Sinn Fein, whose followers destroyed his manuscript of *A History of the Growth of Toleration* in four volumes, which Bury had read and approved. He was the author of many books and articles, especially in encyclopaedias. He died November 2, 1947.

[2] This lecture is now available in a paperback, *The Varieties of History,* edited by Fritz Stern, Meridian Books M37, pp. 209–223.

trine that though history 'may supply material for literary art or philosophical speculations, she is herself simply a science, no less and no more.' " But Bury was no Comtean positivist, and he recognized that history can be interpreted as "a movement of reason." Nevertheless, "it is patent on the face of history that its course has constantly been shaped and modified by the wills of individuals, which are by no means always the expression of the collective will; and that the appearance of such personalities at the given moments is not the necessary outcome of the conditions and cannot be deduced."[3]

Bury "utterly disbelieved in the inevitable." Take for example the fall of the Roman Empire (he had produced the great modern edition of Gibbon in seven volumes, 1896–1900), which has been explained and accounted for in a wide variety of ways by different authors. In Canon Murray's eloquent summary, set forth in his Memoir, Bury "rejects all general explanations . . . , beginning with Gibbon's 'principle of decay,' which demands an explanation. He affirms that the collapse of the Roman power in the west and the success of the barbarians in penetrating and founding States in the provinces were 'the consequences of a series of contingent events,' and these events were the irruption of the Huns, the disaster of Adrianople, the mismanagement of Theodosia, and the inheritance of the Empire by the feeble-minded Honorius. At the same time, he admits that these four events

[3] *Darwin and Modern Science,* p. 538; quoted in the Memoir, p. xxxvii.

need not have led to disaster had it not been for the 'singular misfortune' of Stilicho, who was forced to defend the Empire against Germans without and within its bounds. The causes of the fall of the Roman Empire have been analysed by many investigators. Gibbon had laid stress on the excessive power of the army in the early Empire and on the partial dissolution of its strength at the beginning of the fourth century by the policy of Constantine. He had also noticed the deterioration of the discipline in the army as a main cause of the fall of the Empire, and, of course, to him Christianity had powerfully assisted. Seeley had insisted on the importance of the decline in population, which Bury had shown to be erroneous. Seeck had thought that a general consciousness of the degeneration of the world made men less inclined to propagate the race, and thus intensified the disease. Men suffered from what Bury in another connexion termed loss of nerve. He had also offered the view that the best individuals in Italy were effectually extirpated by the terrible proscriptions which are associated with the names of Sulla and the Triumvirs. Hodgkin had set out under six heads his efficient causes, and they were the foundation of Constantinople, Christianity, slavery, the free distribution of corn [i.e. grain], which pauperised the Roman proletariat, the destruction of the middle class, and barbarous finance.

"The views of Gibbon and Seeley, of Seeck and Hodgkin, are swept to one side, and we are asked to replace them by four contingent causes. No doubt history is a science, yet it is a science in which the casual as well as the causal takes its due share. No one was clearer than Bury that the course of history has been deflected by accident and the presence of genius. Was Gibbon right in his belief that if Charles Martel had been defeated at Tours the creed of Islam would have overspread the greater part of Europe? If Mohammed had been killed in one of the first battles he fought, would a great monotheistic creed have arisen in Arabia? What turn would events have taken if Alexander, the son of Philip of Macedon, had been as incompetent as Commodus, the son of Marcus Aurelius? In the spring of 323 B.C. the control of the framework of civilisation, from the Adriatic to the Punjab, rested upon the single will of Alexander. He was snatched away, and the union, perhaps premature, of East and West passed away with him. What form would French art have assumed had not Charles VIII set out on his expedition to Italy, thereby making France feel the influence of Giotto, the founder of modern painting? It is easy to speak of the inevitable working of cause, course, and consequence, but is it true? Had Frederick the Great never lived, would Prussia have begun the war of 1740, which started the country on the career which made the World War possible?''

Quid ergo Athenis et Hierosolymis?[4] At least, what has Athens to do with *Jerusalem*? What can a purely secular, scientific, skeptical historian contribute toward the elucidation of papal history, and especially that of the First Vatican Council? Much every way! A historian who declined to accept

[4] Tertullian, *De Praescriptione* 7.

determinism ("the inevitable"), and who followed von Ranke's standard of *Geschichte wie es eigentlich gewesen*—history as it actually took place—will surely shed a flood of special illumination upon the scene. And this is what we shall see in the book before us.

BIBLIOGRAPHICAL NOTE

Baynes, Norman H. *John Bagnall Bury, 1861–1927*. London, British Academy, Vol. XIII. This memoir was enlarged and revised in a fuller volume.

———. *A Bibliography of the Works of J. B. Bury, compiled with a Memoir by Norman H. Baynes,* Cambridge Univ. Press, 1929.

Unfortunately, the *Bibliography* does not include the present work, which appeared soon after, though reference might have been made to it, as it was already known that Canon Murray was at work preparing it for publication (see first edition of the present volume, 1930, p. vi). The lectures on the papacy are mentioned by Mr Baynes (p. 50), who states that Bury's lectures as a rule "appealed to few." One course which he frequently delivered was that on the Barbarian Invasions. Now and then he lectured on historical sources and their interpretation, and the methods of modern historical criticism. One of these courses was the series that lies before us. When asked why he chose to offer it, Bury replied that the "History of the Papacy in the Nineteenth Century" was "one side of the History of Freedom of Thought," in which he was deeply interested and on which he published an important book in 1914.

Another noteworthy volume was the *Selected Essays of J. B. Bury,* edited with a valuable introduction by Harold Temperley, Cambridge Univ. Press, 1930. It contains a striking frontispiece, the photograph of Professor Bury made by Lafayette Ltd. The appendix is an extract from the *Quarterly Review,* Vol. CXCII, No. 383, pp. 146–55, which sets forth Bury's earlier views on the Causes of the Survival of the Roman Empire in the East—views which he later modified.

INTRODUCTION

There are in English two outstanding accounts of the First Vatican Council which appeared simultaneously, in 1930. One is the work before us. The other is *The Vatican Council, 1869–1870,* by Dom Cuthbert Butler of Downside Abbey. It is a fully detailed, well documented narrative based on Bishop Ullathorne's letters. Ullathorne was Bishop of Birmingham, a member of the Council, and a letter-writer of the old school, who wrote letters—really epistles!—week by week to his friends in England. He was "a plain straightforward Yorkshire man," says Dom Cuthbert, "of high character, with wide experience of men and affairs, shrewd and intelligent. At the Council he took up and maintained a 'moderate' or middle position, holding aloof from all movements, all intrigues outside the Council Chamber, refusing to act with any party, or to sign any petition, protest, or other document whatsoever; yet closely in touch with leading bishops on both sides. Thus we have in him probably a witness as well informed, and as independent, impartial, and objective, as could well be found."[1]

It is an immense advantage to the student, even now, more than thirty years later, to have these

[1] *The Vatican Council 1869–1870,* Fontana edition 1962, p. 9. See also p. 226.

two books, both extremely objective but from entirely different points of view. They can be compared in detail, and each will be found to support the other. For both authors, the Regius Professor of Modern History and the learned Abbot of Downside—and also his chief authority, Bishop William Bernard Ullathorne—were calm, dispassionate historians, clear-eyed and objective. If often one supplies what the other lacks (for example Professor Bury's description of the mind and character of Pope Pius IX), this is not to be attributed to personal preference or prejudice, or a love of anecdote or gossip: it is a legitimate part of the story. No protesting cry of "irrelevant, immaterial, and misleading" made by the opposing counsel can silence the testimony. Nor is it needful to do so! A perfectly orthodox defense is at hand: God uses strange minds and tongues to utter divine words—as St Paul observed, and long before St Paul the prophet Isaiah (I Corinthians 14.21; Isaiah 28.11). Both modern writers, Bury and Butler, have made thorough and careful use of the available sources, Abbot Butler being even more wide-ranging, it seems, in his use of them than Professor Bury. This is especially true of the use made of the five volumes in Mansi's *Collectio Conciliorum* (vols. 49–53, published in 1923–27), which came out long after Bury's lectures and rather late for Murray's edition of them. Both authors describe the background of the Council, and the events that led up to it: Butler more concerned with the Papal Supremacy, the Temporal Power, with Gallicanism, Ultramontanism, and the New Ultramontanism (as he calls it); Bury more deeply concerned with the *Syllabus of Errors* and the accompanying *Encyclical* (December 8, 1864), both of which he studies in detail, as providing alike the motive for the Council, from the standpoint of Pope Pius, and also the immediate background of the definition of Papal Infallibility. Both describe in detail the opposition, and its defeat—and also the consequences. Both recount the collapse of the temporal power and the triumphant occupation of Rome by the Italian army—and again the consequences. Neither author writes *ex parte,* but as an impartial, objective historian, confident that truth will prevail in the end: *Magna est veritas, et praevalet* (1 Esdras 4.41). And truth is best served by those who follow it faithfully every step of the way, concealing nothing, accusing no one, excusing none. This is the way history should be written.

The full background of both Vatican Councils, Vatican I in 1869–70 and Vatican II in 1962ff, extends much farther back than the beginning of the nineteenth century. It reaches back at least to the sixteenth century, with its catastrophic Reformation and Counter Reformation. The seventeenth century was a dull period, by contrast, in spite of—or partly, perhaps largely, because of—the Thirty Years War in northern Europe and the slow advance of Tridentine reforms within the Catholic Church. "Gallicanism" dates from 1682, when the French clergy declared their four "propositions": (1) the independence of earthly sovereigns in temporal matters, (2) the necessity of conciliar support to render the papal authority valid, (3) the limitations of papal power within the Kingdom of France, and (4) the fallibility of papal judgments when unsupported by the judgment of the Church. On the other hand, the increasing influence of the Jesuits is easily discernible (their centenary was celebrated in 1640), though their influence was not always inspired by the highest motives. The conflict with modern science, which really dates from the seventeenth century, is illustrated by the condemnation of Galileo Galilei (1633). It was also the century of the Jansenists and Port Royal, of Pascal and Molinos, of Madame Guyon and Archbishop Fenelon. In Great Britain it was the century of the Civil War, the Commonwealth, and the Restoration, of the "Glorious Revolution" of 1688 and the Act of Toleration in 1689.

The eighteenth century was the age of Deism and the Aufklärung, of the full-grown influence of Montaigne, Descartes, Hobbes, Spinoza, Pierre Bayle, and Leibniz; it was the age of Hume and Rousseau, of the Pietists, of Frederick the Great and Voltaire, of Lessing, Herder, and Kant, of Schiller and Goethe, and of the American and French Revolutions. None of these names suggests much that sounds favorable to the Church of Rome, whose Popes, from Clement XI in 1700 to Pius VI (1775–1799), were concerned on the whole with advancing the interests of the Church politically and numerically, sometimes by oppression and forcible conversion and especially by winning the allegiance of the nobility. The missionary work of the Church suffered a sharp decline, and for years the Jesuits were in silent revolt against the Curia. Eventually they were driven from Portugal and its colonies (e.g. Paraguay and Brazil), and from France, from Spain, from the Kingdom of Naples and the Duchy of Parma. Finally, in 1773, the Pope, Clement XIV, was compelled to issue a letter (Breve), *Dominus ac Redemptor noster* (Mirbt 548), forever disbanding the Jesuit Order! This was the climax of their undoing—decades of misdirected zeal and energy had led them to undertake an armed revolt of the Indians in Paraguay. Its collapse was the end of their influence in that country and in Portugal. Similarly, the bankruptcy of a mercantile organization operated by a Jesuit on the island of Martinique led to a French crisis: Parlement, to which they had appealed, directed the Jesuits to satisfy the creditors of the insolvent firm and to abandon all commercial activities. Louis XV did his best to save the Order by reform, but in 1764 it was ordered to leave the country. The other Bourbon monarchs followed suit.

In Germany the renewal and spread of "Episcopalism," a movement as old as the Council of Constance and one which easily took on secular and political connotations, and in Austria the rise of "Josephinism" somewhat weakened the influence of the Roman Catholic Church in these two countries; while in France the whole vast crisis of the Revolution and the rise of Napoleon Bonaparte seemed to mark the end of an era. To many, it marked the end of the Catholic Church and the Christian religion. But Napoleon could not afford to let the Church collapse, as he needed it for political purposes; and by the Concordat of July 15, 1801 the Church was restored, not as the state religion but as the religion of the majority of French citizens.

This marked the very nadir of the Church's fortunes in France; but it also marked the turning point and the beginning of a movement of recovery. After successive reversals and a series of slow starts, this finally got under way in the opening decades of the following century. The collapse of the Church in France affected the Church in other lands, e.g. in Germany, where its traditional privileges, under the old German Empire, were revoked (1803) and the ecclesiastical principalities brought to an end. It also brought about the end of the Holy Roman Empire of the German Nation (1806), a fiction, but a powerful one, which had dominated much of the West for at least eight and a half centuries, since Otto the Great, and more likely for ten, since Charlemagne.

The new day that now dawned was announced by all the trumpets and artillery of the skies, by all the apocalyptic thunders and lightnings which had been loosed, near and far, by the French Revolution. It was a time of revolt and unrest, and so continued for several decades. The Congress of Vienna (in 1815) did not settle much. Like other "peace conferences" it left undone as much as it accomplished. In fact it unsettled much, and also left an old imbalance that led to constant friction and tension and eventually set the scene for two world wars. Before the middle of the nineteenth century, a whole series of revolutions took place, as if lighted from the earlier fuse of France in 1789. The uprisings in Spain (1820) and Italy (1820–21); the wars of liberation in South America (1814–29); the Greek War of Independence (1821–29); the July Revolution in Paris (1830), followed by disturbances in Belgium, Poland, Italy, and in parts of Germany; the February Revolution in Paris (1848)—all these led up to the great crisis of 1848–52 which resulted in the expulsion of liberals and radicals in many quarters and the triumph of reaction. A new kingdom arose in Italy, a new empire in Germany. Even Russia, the Balkans, and Turkey were upset; one can trace the sparking fuse to its final conflagrations even later —in 1905, 1908, 1909, 1914, 1918, perhaps even 1938 and 1939. Socialism was widely advocated. It was the era of Saint-Simon, Proudhon, Robert Owen, Marx and Engels. Rousseau's influence had finally come to fruition, and with it the anti-Christian, anti-religious, anti-ecclesiastical feelings and convictions of the Aufklärung.

To meet all this intellectual turmoil and social upheaval and disaster, the Church was still as unprepared as it had been in the eighteenth century; it was still mediaeval in outlook, still baroque in manners and ideas and grasp of political and moral situations, still blind to the steadily mounting crisis of modernity—modern science, modern skepticism, historicism, rationalism, naturalism, and nationalism. When one reviews the development of European thought during this period, in philosophy, in science, in letters, in art, it is difficult to see how the Roman Catholic Church, i.e. the papacy, could have come to terms with it (as many modern writers have advocated). What possible terms could the Church devise as a *modus vivendi* in close association with groups which seemed to deny every principle for which Christianity stood? It is discouraging to read the *Syllabus of Errors*;

yet one can only admire the plucky ecclesiastics who drew it up, and the Pope who was ready to take on a whole world of opposition and to breast a broad sea of troubles. From our standpoint, decades later, it looks as if it must have been a hopeless challenge; yet conditions within the Church warranted more optimism than we realize. From 1800 to 1846 stretched almost half a century, with four Popes: Pius VII (1800–23), Leo XII (1823–29), Pius VIII (1829–30), Gregory XVI (1831–46). During these four pontificates the Church succeeded in rallying its forces and unfurling its banners. By 1815 the political menace of Napoleon was removed, and Europe, including the Church, could breathe more freely. The Papal States were now restored to the Church by the Congress of Vienna, with their old boundaries, and the running conflict with social radicalism, atheism, skepticism, and all ideas born of the French Revolution seemed to have taken a turn for the better and to be approaching a conclusion. Pius VII was especially firm in attacking these anti-religious ideas. But his chief difficulty had been with Napoleon, who in 1809 seized the Papal States and ordered the Pope to be taken into custody. Pius was first transported to Grenoble and later to Savona on the Gulf of Genoa, where he was deprived of all books and writing materials. Three years later Napoleon prepared to liberate him, i.e. to leave him unguarded at Fontainebleau where the English might rescue him. But in 1814 the allies forced Napoleon to liberate the Pope and restore the States of the Church. The pendulum swung back, and the Jesuits were restored, the Index and the

Inquisition revived. It was a natural if extreme reversal of a dangerous trend; and it had been the resolute courage of one man that saved the Church from a tyrant's domination.

The three Popes who succeeded Pius were equally firm in their rejection of modern radical ideas. The *Index of Forbidden Books* was enlarged to include the works of many modern historians and philosophers; all anti-Catholic secret societies were proscribed, especially the Free Masons; Bible societies also fell under the ban, even the Catholic Bible Societies; the education of the clergy was removed from secular universities to cloistered seminaries from which all modern ideas were to be excluded. The Jesuit Order was restored once more by the Bull *Sollicitudo omnium ecclesiarum* (August 7, 1814)[2] and began at once the prodigious expansion in numbers and influence which has characterized it ever since. It has become the leading religious order in the Roman Catholic Church, and has been of immense service to the papacy, under whose explicit direction it functions. Treaties and "Concordats" were established with various nations and great powers. By 1823 the Church had recovered all lost ground in its political relations. The new era saw an enormous expansion in missionary activity, which increased steadily throughout the nineteenth century and is still in full swing, despite the terrible setbacks suffered during two world wars and the revolutions and revolts that followed them. At the same time, the development

[2] See the text in Mirbt, *Quellen zur Geschichte des Papsttums*, 4th ed., no. 564.

of modern papalism, in both theory and practice, may clearly be traced to the period after 1815. The papacy is no longer centered in the personal prestige of an ecclesiastical monarch, but in a great world-organization whose axis and powerhouse is located in Rome; and its policies are tempered to the needs of mankind, rather than adjusted to the interests of a tiny ecclesiastical monarchy embracing a few square miles of territory in the heart of the Italian peninsula.

Such was the general background of the First Vatican Council, which occupies the center of the stage in Professor Bury's lectures. He begins with the *Syllabus of Errors* (1864) and ends with the fall of the Temporal Power (1870). We must now examine the foreground, and the steps that led directly to the Council. This foreground has two levels, the immediate and foremost being the demand for a restored and reunited Italy, the more remote the movement toward a reunited Germany.

In Italy the *Risorgimento* was already under way. Austria had been given Lombardy and Venezia by the Congress of Vienna. Piedmont belonged to the Kingdom of Sardinia. Parma, Modena, and the Grand Duchy of Tuscany were independent. The Papal States stretched diagonally across the middle of the peninsula, from the mouth of the Po to Terracina south of Rome. The Kingdom of the Two Sicilies included the rest. The beginning of the movement toward reunion had been the growing opposition to Austrian occupation of the North and North East, though it was not at all clear which plan of restoration was the best, whether a federation of states headed by the papacy, a "deal" with the King of Sardinia, or a new republic—the last was Mazzini's plan. As the historian Henry Littlefield observes, it was characteristic of the liberal movement in Italy that it ignored social liberalism, and concentrated on an intense enthusiasm for nationalism. The industrial revolution had not yet influenced agrarian and rural Italy as it had, with transforming energy, the populace of England and France.[3] Nevertheless, the opposition to Austria had been latent for a long time before the *Risorgimento,* ever since the 17th century, as is clearly illustrated by the plot of Alessandro Manzoni's great novel, *I Promessi Sposi* (1825). The 1848 revolution which shook all of Europe had its effects in Italy also. The rebellion centered in Milan, and the Austrian garrisons were driven out of Lombardy and Venezia. At once the choice of a plan was made final without any further discussion: Charles Albert, the King of Sardinia and Piedmont, declared war on Austria and came to the defense of the revolutionists. But the Austrians rallied and Charles Albert was defeated the following year, resigned the throne, and was succeeded by his able son Victor Emmanuel II.

For ten years the kettle simmered. Then Cavour's wily strategy of provocation led the Austrians to demand that Sardinia disarm and cease encouraging revolution in northern Italy—an ultimatum that Cavour had prepared for: the French were now on the scene, and the combined French and Sardinian forces defeated the Austrians at

[3] See Henry Littlefield, *History of Europe since 1815,* p. 33.

Magenta and Solferino. Immediately the other north Italian states revolted and overthrew their Hapsburg rulers. Alas, the promises of Napoleon III were not binding; as he learned of the German mobilization across the Rhine, his intention of freeing all Italy "from the Alps to the Adriatic" suddenly vanished. Victor Emmanuel could hardly continue the war alone, and so Cavour bribed Napoleon with an offer of Savoy and Nice, if he would approve the annexation of Modena, Parma, Romagna, and Tuscany by the King of Sardinia. This was agreed. Meanwhile, Giuseppe Garibaldi was uniting the Two Sicilies and Naples with the proposed new government of Italy—in his view it was to be a republic. In 1860 Victor Emmanuel defeated the papal army at Castelfidardo, and took over the whole papal territory except the immediate area around Rome. Venezia was not taken from Austria until 1866, at the end of the Seven Weeks War; but the rest of Italy, except for the vastly reduced southwest corner of the Papal States, was incorporated in the new Kingdom of Italy. Its king was Victor Emmanuel II, and its Parliament met in Turin, which was in Piedmont, part of the old Kingdom of Sardinia. Savoy and Nice had been lost to France, and Napoleon III still defended the Pope in his tiny territory. But the day was not far distant when the defense would be withdrawn, and the only vestige of the old States of the Church would be the Vatican itself and a few surrounding acres.

This event requires a look at the second stage of the immediate foreground of the Council, namely the events in Germany. For several generations, even before the end of the Holy Roman Empire in 1806, Germany had been broken up into a vast collection of tiny states—over three hundred in the early 18th century. These had been combined into thirty-eight by 1815. The slow process of amalgamation and union was aided by public opinion, e.g. as swayed by the oratory of the philosopher Fichte, who delivered his famous Lectures to the German Nation (*Reden an die Deutsche Nation*) in 1807–08. Naturally the situation called for a leader. That leader was found in the largest of the German states, Prussia, which extended from Tilsit and Königsberg near the Baltic Sea to the Austrian border, in the East, and included Berlin, destined to be the capital of the new Germany. Moreover, the population of Prussia was almost solidly German, and had already taken a decisive part in the wars against Napoleon. The King of Prussia, William I (1861–88), was a militarist, and a "strong" leader. His Prime Minister, Otto von Bismarck (1815–1898), was given a free hand in "curbing" the Prussian Parliament, in framing a budget and collecting taxes. He enjoyed the title, "the iron chancellor," and followed a policy of "blood and iron" rather than political maneuvering and persuasion. His first step was to take over Schleswig-Holstein (in 1864), which led at once to the Seven Weeks War with Austria, which in turn crowded Austria out of the competition for leadership in the projected new German Empire. The whole policy of Metternich, who had dominated the Congress of Vienna in 1815 and favored Austria (which was Catholic) as against all Catholic and Protestant states farther north, was now completely blocked. A liberal movement in Austria aimed at a degree of independence, but it was swallowed up in the *Ausgleich* (1867) which followed the battle of Sadowa. Only the southern states were now left free—especially Saxony, Bavaria, Württemberg, Baden, and the Palatinate. Napoleon III endeavored to stem the tide of German expansion, and sought to gain the territory of the Palatinate, which now belonged to Bavaria. Failing in this, he next asked for Belgium and Luxemburg. His colossal effrontery only alarmed and angered the remaining German princes: here was another Napoleon, true to his name! He even tried to annex Poland, a Catholic country, and free it from Russia; and to attach Mexico to the French "empire"—a step which failed as soon as the American Civil War had ended and the Monroe Doctrine could be firmly restated. Finally, Napoleon protested against the coronation of a Hohenzollern in Spain, following the expulsion of Isabella II (1869). The tricky Bismarck had led him into a trap: he knew that Napoleon would object to a German king on his southern flank, matching the vastly increased power of the German realm in the east. Napoleon protested in a telegram to King William, and the king sent on the message to Bismarck, who cleverly and unscrupulously altered it in such a way as to arouse flaming antagonism among the people of both France and Prussia. The French at once declared war, and the South German states joined Prussia in preparation to resist.

The result for France of the brief Franco-Prussian War of 1870 was a total defeat, the loss of Alsace-Lorraine, the imposition of a billion dollar indemnity, and an army of occupation in French territory until the debt was paid. The result for Germany was the triumph of Bismarck's ruthless policies: the union of all Germany, including the new territories of Alsace and Lorraine, and the establishment of the new German Empire (1871), with the King of Prussia the first emperor of the new Reich. The result for Italy and the papacy can be briefly told. In preparation for the invasion of Germany (there was no thought of defending France—the maps issued to the French soldiers showed only the German territory to be taken!), Napoleon withdrew his troops from Rome. At once the army of Victor Emmanuel II marched in, and the last fragment of papal territory was absorbed by the new Kingdom of Italy. The Pope retained the Vatican Palace and St Peter's, the Vatican Gardens and Castel Gandolfo, and received a compensatory amount in capital and an annual royalty—which last (both the lump sum and the annual payment) he resolutely and in principle declined. It was the darkest hour. After fourteen centuries, ever since Gregory the Great, centuries during which kings and emperors, princes and potentates had stood outside the papal gates to solicit counsel and advice, or decrees and decisions, or aid and support, the papacy was now politically insignificant. The great contest in the North, between the rising modern powers now locked in deadly strife, paid no attention to the needs of Italy or the Pope, which were like the small boys at the end of a vicious "crack the whip": they came last and suffered most.

After considering the movements and events of the half-century preceding Vatican I, it is easier to understand the conservatism and even reaction of Pope Pius and the Council. There had been numerous attempts, ever since the Council of Trent, to list and reject the "errors of the day"—for example Pope Pius V's denunciation of the errors of Michael Baius (1567; see Denzinger 1901–80), or Innocent X's constitution against Cornelius Jansen (1653; Denz. 2001–07), or Alexander VII's condemnation of lax moral teaching in 1665 (Denz. 2021–65), followed by Innocent XI's condemnations in 1679 (Denz. 2101–67) and his list of the errors of the Quietists in 1687 (Denz. 2201–69); there were also Alexander VIII's rejection of Jansenism (1690; Denz. 2301–32), Innocent XII's rejection of Archbishop Fénelon's errors (1699; Denz. 2351–74), Clement XI's rejection of the errors of Paschasius Quesnel (1713; Denz. 2400–2502), Gregory XVI's condemnation of Fideism (1840; Denz. 2751–56), and Pius IX's own condemnation of errors in 1846 (Denz. 2775–86)—all these lists of condemned errors, and more, which fill many pages of Denzinger's *Enchiridion Symbolorum,* reflect the attitude of apprehension, of alarm, and of antagonism and negation which seemed to be the only reaction of the Popes to the rising tide of modern thought. For the supreme teachers of Christendom to do nothing more than condemn error was one of the saddest tragedies in modern history. It convinced millions of intelligent persons outside the Roman Catholic Church that the papacy had nothing to offer the modern world.

A further blow was the Bull *Ineffabilis Deus,* issued in 1854 (Denzinger 2800–04; Mirbt 596; Bettenson 381f). It set forth a definition of the doctrine of the Immaculate Conception of the Blessed Virgin Mary, together with a warning against any publicly expressed doubt or denial. It read:

"To the honor of the Holy and Undivided Trinity, to the glory and adornment of the Virgin Mother of God, to the exaltation of the Catholic Faith and the increase of the Christian religion, We, with the authority of our Lord Jesus Christ, the Blessed Apostles Peter and Paul, and with our own [authority], declare, pronounce, and define that the doctrine which holds that the Most Blessed Virgin Mary, in the first instant of her conception, was, by a singular grace and privilege of Almighty God, preserved untouched by any taint of original guilt, in consideration of the merits of Christ Jesus the Savior of mankind—[we declare] that [this doctrine] was revealed by God and therefore is to be firmly and steadfastly believed by all the faithful.

"Wherefore, if any shall presume (which may God forbid!) to think in their hearts anything contrary to this definition of Ours, let them realize and well know that they have been condemned by their own judgment, have suffered shipwreck concerning the faith, and have broken away from the unity of the Church; and that besides all this they subject themselves to the lawful penalties, if they dare to signify, by word or in writing or by any other external means, what they think in their hearts."

Hitherto, the doctrine of the Immaculate Conception had been, for centuries, a "pious opinion," and was debated only by theologians, and then on grounds chiefly metaphysical, logical, or those of congruity. The blessed Body which bore the sacred Body of God the Son, when He became incarnate, could not be thought to have been sinful, i.e. tainted by original sin, which infects all human nature descended from Adam. After the Middle Ages, the dogma had moved slowly toward definition. In 1483 Pope Sixtus IV censured those who opposed it (Denz. 1425–26). But it was an unprecedented step for a pope to define a dogma, without consultation with a council, and to issue the decree in a Bull. In lieu of a council, Pius had consulted the universal episcopate (February 2, 1849); of 603 bishops interrogated, 546 replied favorably. In the minds of Protestants this method of procedure did not rouse so much objection as the whole act of "adding to the Christian Faith." The judgment of Henry Bettenson is widely shared: "The promulgation of the dogma was one of the fruits of that Ultramontanism, encouraged by the restored Jesuits, which in the pontificate of Pius IX produced also the Syllabus of Errors and the Decree of Infallibility."[4] It was also, no doubt, like the *Syllabus*, a product of the general reaction which the unchecked growth of "liberalism" in the first half of the century had provoked in the minds of traditionalists and of those whose devotions included—or culminated in—prayers to and medita-

[4] *Documents of the Christian Church,* 2d ed., 1963, p. 381.

tions upon the Blessed Virgin. "To the law and to the testimony!" Let the Church gird up its loins, and prepare for the worst! Let the weak spots in the undefined areas of the faith, and the positive errors in its interpretation, be covered and defended! In the mind of a pope like Pius IX, with the unhappy early experiences of liberalism he had suffered, it was no wonder that the best safeguard of the Christian faith was a Maginot Line of impenetrable defense. The decree won the approval of many in the East, where Marian devotions were —and are—popular. But it further alienated almost the whole of the Protestant world, and also the multitude of non-churchmen who were now coming increasingly under the influence of modern science. As poetry, as pious opinion, as an inspiration of a deep and spiritual type of devotion, it was tolerable—for those who believed in religious toleration. But as a statement of one of the cardinal doctrines of the Christian faith, something *de fide,* a doctrine "necessary to salvation," it went altogether too far.

But this blow was followed by more—the *Syllabus of Errors* and the Infallibility Decree. Here is the point at which Professor Bury took up the tale, in his surviving lectures. The text of the *Syllabus* may be found in Denzinger 2901–80 or Mirbt 602; abridged in Bettenson, pp. 382–84. The text of the Decree is in Denzinger 3065–75; Mirbt 606; Bettenson 384f. For the *Quanta cura* (Bury, p. 1), see Denzinger 2890–96. And see the earlier encyclical, *Qui pluribus,* dated November 9, 1846, at the beginning of the pope's reign, in Denzinger 2775–86.

Gregory XVI's *Mirari vos arbitramur* (August 15, 1832) is quoted in Denzinger 2730–32 and Mirbt 583. For the dogmatic constitution *Pastor Aeternus* (Bury p. 128), see Denzinger 3050–75.[5]

FREDERICK C. GRANT

Union Theological Seminary
New York, June 1964.

[5] The reader should note that the index to this volume supplies fuller names and titles than are found in Bury's footnotes.

HISTORY OF THE PAPACY IN THE 19TH CENTURY

I

THE SYLLABUS

WHEN the temporal power of the Papacy was tottering to its fall, in consequence of the Liberal movement and the political ability of the Sardinian Government, Pius IX. flung down the gauntlet of challenge and defiance to Nineteenth Century civilisation. His immediate predecessors, in their conflict with liberalism, had issued Encyclical Letters condemning modern doctrines; but even the fulminations of Gregory XVI.'s *Mirari vos*[1] were taken quietly and rather as a matter of course. Not so the *Quanta Cura* of Pius IX. and the Syllabus of Errors which accompanied it. Appearing thirty-two years later than the *Mirari vos*, it struck with amazement a generation which was so much further away from the days of the Holy Alliance. With the majority of educated people in Europe, the liberal ideas which were winning their victory about 1830 had already become commonplaces, and they were astonished by a drastic and authoritative reminder that the Papacy was as mediaeval as ever in its attitude to modern society and civilisation, and uncompromis-

[1] It was read on the Feast of the Assumption of the Virgin Mary, August 15, 1832, *Bullarium Romanum*, xix. pp. 126 f. In French in *Sylvain*, pp. 362 f.

ingly hostile to the ideas which commanded the assent of the most civilised sections of mankind.

The originator of the idea of cataloguing and condemning modern errors was not Pius IX., but his successor Leo XIII. At the Council of Spoleto in 1849, Pecci, then Bishop of Perugia, proposed that the Council should request the Pope to condemn the most flagrant errors of the day respecting the authority of the Church and the rights of property. It was characteristic that he should have initiated this idea, concerning as it did, not theology, but politics and civilisation. When he was elected Pope in 1878, Gambetta remarked that he was more a diplomatist than a priest. The idea recommended itself to the Jesuits; and in 1851 the central organ of ultramontanism, the *Civiltà Catholica*,[1] suggested that it would be wise to issue a condemnation of modern errors, simultaneously with the promulgation of the doctrine of the Immaculate Conception, for which preparations were then being made. Cardinal Fornari was directed by the Pope to ask the opinions of prelates and other Catholic leaders on this question; and the result was that it was deemed advisable to issue a list of errors in conjunction with a special Bull, and not connect it with the Bull on the Immaculate Conception. The Commission which had been appointed to prepare the latter Bull, when its work was over, was turned on to consider the subject of

[1] Friedrich, *Geschichte des vatikanischen Konzils*, i. pp. 502-4. On the Jesuit agitation and the liberal opposition cf. Frommann, *Geschichte u. Kritik des vatikanischen Concils von 1869 u. 1870*, pp. 13-21. Cf. *Encyclique* (of Pius IX.) *aux évêques d'Italie, texte lat. avec trad. franç.*, etc., by G. Mazzini. Cf. also *Historische Zeitschrift*, v. p. 563 (1908).

the errors, and it worked till 1860. It included the learned Thenier, as well as Passaglia, Schrader, and Perrone.[1]

In 1860 Bishop Gerbet of Perpignan issued a Pastoral Instruction to the clergy of his diocese, in which he enumerated a series of 85 erroneous doctrines, of socialistic or rationalistic nature.[2] It caught the attention of the Pope, and a larger Commission was appointed, which made Gerbet's list a basis to work on. This body produced in 1862 a catalogue of 61 theses, with corresponding theological censures; and this was laid before a council of bishops which had been summoned for another purpose at Rome. In an Allocution, *Maxima quidem*, in June of this year, the Pope condemned these theses, and the assembled Bishops assented to the Papal condemnation. But in October a Turin paper, *Il Mediatore*, published the text of the list, which had been hitherto kept secret. It created a sensation and called forth the remonstrances of Liberal Catholics. Dupanloup, the Bishop of Orleans, urged that it was inopportune.[3] The effects of this premature disclosure induced the Pope to postpone and modify his action. He appointed a new Commission, under the presidency of Luigi Bilio, which prepared the final list of 80 errors, which included 30 of the former 61; but the theological censures were omitted. It was published, with a special En-

[1] Hettinger, *Aus Welt u. Kirche*, i. pp. 106 ff.

[2] Richard, *Gerbet et Salinis*, pp. 172 ff.

[3] For opposed estimates of his career contrast Lagrange's appreciation with Maynard's depreciation. Cf. Lagrange, *Vie de Mgr. Dupanloup*, i. pp. 278 ff., and especially ii. p. 474; Pfülf, *Mgr. v. Ketteler*, iii. pp. 3 ff.; Pelletier, *Dupanloup*, p. 96.

cyclical, on December 8, 1864, and had the incidental significance of appearing as a sort of reply to the September Convention[1] between Italy and France, which had caused great indignation at Rome.

It is important to observe that the ultramontanes strongly desired the issue of the *Syllabus* for the special reason that it would be a weapon against the Liberal Catholics. The old leader, Montalembert, read papers at a religious Congress at Malines on the text of a Free Church in a Free State. They moved the ultramontane Bishop Pie of Poitiers to appeal to Pius IX. to take measures against the author of such heretical pronouncements in regard to the liberty of belief.[2] It was an offence to the Pope that this doctrine, which Cavour had wished to realise in Italy, should be preached at a Catholic Assembly. His reply to Bishop Pie intimated this, and admitted the principle that freedom of conscience should be asserted in countries (like Russia and Sweden) where Catholics were in a minority, but not in Catholic lands.[3] After this Pie had issued two manifestoes in the course of 1864, to prepare the way for the *Syllabus*.[4]

The Encyclical letter which was sent out to the Catholic prelates along with the *Syllabus* provides the condemnation *in globo* of the classes of errors which the *Syllabus* enumerates *singulatim*. The leading ideas which are associated closely with modern progress are described as *monstrosa opi-*

[1] Nielsen, *History of the Papacy in the Nineteenth Century*, ii. pp. 251-2. On the true inwardness of this Convention cf. Thouvenel's remarkable *Le Secret de l'Empereur*.

[2] Baunard, *Le Cardinal Pie*, ii. p. 214.

[3] *Ibid.* ii. p. 215.

[4] *Ibid.* ii. pp. 223 ff.

nionum portenta, and those who propagate them are designated as slaves of corruption who design to demolish society, *civilis societatis fundamenta convellere.*[1] The head and front of their offending is that they would hinder and remove "that salutary force" which the Catholic Church ought to exercise not only on individuals but on nations, peoples, and governments. After a preface, to this effect, on the general iniquity of the *Zeitgeist*, the Pope goes on to signalise what he calls the "impious and absurd principle of naturalism", which means that "the highest interests of public society and civil progress require that society should be governed without taking account of religion, as if it did not exist, or at least without recognising any difference between the true and false religion", and that "that State is best which declines to acknowledge the obligation of punishing violators of the Catholic religion except so far as public order demands". Thus the Pope uses the term "naturalism" to include toleration and secularism; it is, in fact, the antithesis of the mediaeval order. He begins his comments on this doctrine by quoting with approval a passage from the *Mirari vos* of his predecessor, where liberty of conscience and the right of each man to practise his own religion are described as *deliramentum*. Such liberty, says Pius, citing St. Augustine, is *libertas perditionis*. He then produces an argument. If you take away religion from the fabric of civil society,

[1] On Pius IX.'s project cf. Maynard, *Dupanloup et M. Lagrange*, p. 134. On the Syllabus cf. Goetz, *Der Ultramontanismus als Weltanschauung auf Grund des Syllabus*. Cf. Mourret, *Le Mouvement catholique en France*, pp. 130-33.

you substitute instead of true justice and lawful right "material force" (*vis materialis*); and that is why some dare to proclaim that the will of the people, when it declares itself, is the supreme law, unbound by any divine or human principles of *jus*, and that in politics *faits accomplis*, "facta consummata", just because they are *consummata*, have legal force. "Who does not see that human society, loosed from the chains of religion and true justice, can have no other aim save that of acquiring and heaping up wealth, and can follow no other law save the desire of serving personal pleasures and interests?" The general drift, you see, of the argument is: liberty, toleration, secularism, and democracy are closely bound together, and what they mean is materialism.

The Encyclical then touches on some particular points in which modern society had revolted against the claims of Ecclesiasticism; first of all, the drastic limitation placed upon religious societies; then the objection to compulsory cessation of work on Sundays; then the assumption by the State of the duty of educating children, a principle which is denounced as communism and socialism. After this it passes to the claims of Canon law to recognition and obedience; it censures the errors that the ecclesiastical laws are only binding in conscience when they are published by the civil power; that the decrees of the Pope in religious and ecclesiastical matters require the confirmation or at least the assent of the civil power; that the apostolic constitutions, which forbid secret societies and excommunicate their members, are not valid where the government tolerates such societies; that the excommunication, pronounced by the Council of Trent and Popes against those who usurp ecclesiastical property, fails to discriminate as it ought between secular and spiritual things, and aims at purely mundane wealth; that the Church ought not to ordain anything to coerce the consciences of the faithful respecting the use of temporal goods; that the Church has no right to discipline offenders against the laws by temporal chastisement [the principle here involved includes death for heretics]; that it is not inconsistent with theology or public law to vindicate for the State the property of goods possessed by Churches, religious societies, and pious institutions. The Pope further condemns the view that the Ecclesiastical *potestas* is not divinely distinct and independent of the civil *potestas*, and that the recognition of an ecclesiastical power independent of the State necessarily means that the sphere of the civil power will be invaded by the Church.

The Encyclical concludes with an expression of confidence in the power of the Immaculate Virgin, who is said to destroy all heresies in the Universe, and is curiously described as standing, on her Son's right hand, in a dress of gold and *circumamicta varietate*, with a cloak of divers colours.

Altogether in this document the Pope has condemned 16 errors; I follow the analysis of ultramontane interpreters. These 16, however, do not include a censure of the freethinkers who deny the divinity of Christ:[1] this is the only theological part

[1] There is implicit censure of Renan's *Vie de Jésus*, published in 1863. Cf. Baunard, *Hist. du card. Pie*, ii. p. 199.

of the Encyclical. Wrapt up in religious phraseology, it is really a political document, setting forth an ideal of civilisation and declaring principles of political import.

The positive principles which it asserts by means of condemning their negations may be summed up thus: The State must recognise a particular religion as regnant, and submit to its influence, and this religion must be the Catholic; the power of the State must be at its disposal, and all who do not conform to its requirements must be compelled or punished. The duty of governments is to protect the Church, and freedom of conscience and cult is madness. Not the popular will, but religion, that is the papal authority, is the basis of civil society, otherwise it will sink into materialism. The Church is superior to the State, and therefore the State has no right to dictate to her, and has no power over religious orders. The family and the education of children belong to the Church, not to the State. The Pope can decree and prescribe what he chooses, without the State's permission, and his authority is not limited to doctrines and morals.

It is of importance to determine the relation of this Encyclical to the *Syllabus*, because the interpretation and the authority of the *Syllabus* are nearly affected by it. Those who wish to explain away the *Syllabus* attempted to disconnect it from the Encyclical. This contention cannot be sustained. I have said that the two documents were distributed to the bishops together, and they were accompanied by a covering letter of Cardinal Antonelli, which is quite decisive. Antonelli says: "The Pope has already in Encyclicals and Allocutions condemned the principal errors of this most unhappy age. But all of you may not have received all the pontifical acts. Therefore the Pope wished a Syllabus of these Errors to be drawn up for the use of all the Catholic bishops that they may have before their eyes the pernicious doctrines that he has proscribed. I therefore send you a printed copy of the Syllabus on the same occasion on which the Pope thought it well to address another Encyclical Epistle to Catholic prelates."[1] This letter leaves no doubt that the *Syllabus* was intended to have a dogmatic value, and to be interpreted in connexion with the *Quanta cura* and the preceding utterances of the Pope on the subject of modern errors. All the ultramontane critics have recognised this connexion. The *Syllabus* is not verbally identical, nor is it conterminous in the compass of its topics with the Encyclical; but it has been pointed out by an ultramontane critic that 41 theses are implied in the Encyclical, and these 41 are the most important. It follows that at least for the condemnation of these 41 theses the same authority must be claimed which belongs to the Encyclical. It is futile for a recent writer,[2] of great learning, who is prominent among the German liberal Catholics, to say that the *Syllabus* has not a dogmatic character, that its scope was merely historical and temporary, that it was no more than a momentary

[1] Rönneke, *Pius IX. Encyklika u. Syllabus,* xiii. The able and astute Cardinal Antonelli was the evil genius of Pius IX., who was a man of most mediocre ability. Cf. Woodward, *Three Studies in European Conservatism,* pp. 296-7.

[2] Ehrhard, *Der Katholizismus u. das zwanzigste Jahrhundert,* pp. 260-65.

counterstroke to defend ecclesiastical authority against the extravagant attacks of the liberals against the Church in the middle of the nineteenth century. Such explanations are only the desperate resorts to which those have to betake themselves who try to reconcile the polar opposites, liberty and papal authority, progress and ecclesiasticism.

Not only liberal Catholics, but ultramontanes when they do not wish to confess the incompatibility of the Church with modern civilisation, have attempted to mitigate the meaning of the *Syllabus*. We shall see afterwards how M. Dupanloup endeavoured to explain it away. We must not allow ourselves to be embarrassed by these devices. We have perfectly sufficient means of securely determining its interpretation. We have in the first place the Encyclical, and in the second the commentaries of various ultramontane writers, who, as the document originated entirely in ultramontane circles and in the ultramontane interest, can be relied on to explain it. And most important among them is the book of the Austrian Jesuit Schrader, who was a member of the first Commission, entitled *Der Papst und die modernen Ideen*.[1] Next to this is the collection of eight studies by different Jesuit writers, which appeared separately in the Jesuit organ *Stimmen aus Maria-Laach*[2] between 1865 and 1869, and were then published in one volume, which build up on the basis of the *Syllabus* a system of theoretical ultramontanism. It is of course very technical, but provision has more recently been made for the popular

[1] Vienna, 1865. Cf. Friedrich, *Geschichte des vatikanischen Konzils*, i. p. 291.

[2] Freiburg im Breisgau, 1869.

diffusion of the principles of the *Syllabus* among German Catholics by a little book of the Jesuit Brors, called "Modern A B C for Catholics of all Classes, Short replies to modern attacks on Catholicism".[1]

As the *Syllabus* states the errors which are to be rejected, in order to obtain the true doctrine, we have to convert the negation into a positive form. And in performing this operation, the ultramontane interpreters lay down that we must take not the logical contrary, but the logical contradictory. As a matter of fact, Schrader has done this for us.[2]

The title at the head of the document runs: "Syllabus embracing the chief errors of our age (*praecipuos nostrae aetatis errores*), which are censured in Consistorial Allocutions, in encyclical and other apostolic letters of our most holy lord Pope Pius IX.". You observe that it is only the chief errors; and although they are not all censured in the pronouncements referred to in the same degree, they are all errors rejected by ultramontane doctrine; and Berlinghieri wrote a book in 1865, which the Pope approved, entitled *The 80 heresies of our age.*[3]

The 80 propositions are divided into 10 subject groups with special headings. The first group is entitled "Pantheism, Naturalism and absolute Rationalism"; the second, "Limited Rationalism".

[1] Berlin, 1902. Its title is *Modernes A B C für Katholiken aller Hände.* As three German editions appeared in 1902, it had a considerable circulation.

[2] In his *Der Papst u. die modernen Ideen.* His *Die Encyclica* forms Heft 2 of his *Der Papst.*

[3] Roberto Berlinghieri, *Le 80 eresie del nostro secolo condannate dalla Santa Romana Chiesa quali si legono nel Sillabo.* Roma, 1872.

The fourteen items of these groups contain the doctrinal foundation for the rest. On the first group we need not linger. It contains theses which were condemned by all pious Christians, as a matter of course; and a month after the publication Döllinger wrote that "a solemn repudiation of these errors by a special pronouncement verges on the comic; it is almost as if Rome were to proclaim that it is wrong and heretical to believe in the divinity of Juno or Apollo, or consider Mohammed a prophet".[1] The criticism would be just if these theses stood by themselves, but from the point of view of the whole document they are not unnecessary or superfluous. The errors here collected all touch the truth of revelation, and as the absolute authority of revelation is the ultimate base of the whole ultramontane system, the document would be not theoretically complete without this portion. The fifth thesis, for instance, is obviously of great importance. It runs: "The divine revelation is imperfect and therefore subject to a continuous and indefinite progress corresponding to the advance of human reason". This is a proposition which nowadays many non-Catholic and some Catholic Christians would assent to. Converting it into the true doctrine, we get: "The divine revelation is not imperfect, and therefore it is not subject to continuous and indefinite progress, corresponding to the advance of human reason". This proposition is indispensable to ultramontane theory.

[1] There is implicit censure of Döllinger, who, in September 1863, had read a paper at Munich on *Die Vergangenheit u. Gegenwart der kath. Theologie* (Kl. Schriften, pp. 161 ff.), and in it he bitterly censures Scholasticism. Döllinger wrote the *Römische Briefe*. In their English form they are entitled "Letters from Rome", by Quirinus.

The second group of errors, under the title Limited (Moderatus) Rationalism, was particularly suggested by doctrines taught in the philosophical works of Professor Frohschammer of Munich.[1] It is important because it sets forth the ultramontane doctrine of the relation of the Church to science. I will reproduce it in the positive form, *i.e.* the propositions which are opposed to the errors.

(1) As human reason cannot be co-equalised with religion, therefore theological studies cannot be treated like philosophical studies.

(2) It is not true that all dogmas of the Christian Church without distinction are the object of natural science (*naturalis scientia*) or philosophy; and human reason cannot, of its own natural powers and principles, attain to the true knowledge of all, even the obscurest dogmas, even if these dogmas are presented to reason as an object.

The point of these two theses is to exclude human reason from religious doctrine, and make this the exclusive domain of theology, or in other words ecclesiastical authority.

(3) We may draw a distinction between the philosopher and philosophy; but the philosopher has not the right or obligation to submit to the authority which he considers true; while philosophy can and must submit itself to authority.

This means the subjection of science to ecclesiastical authority.

(4) The Church may not only at all times take proceedings against philosophy but she may not

[1] Friedrich, pp. 310, 311, 318, 383.

even tolerate the errors of philosophy or leave it to philosophy itself to correct those errors.

This principle implies the institution of the Index.

(5) The decrees of the apostolic Chair and the Roman congregations do not hinder the free progress of science and learning.

This declaration reminds us of the case of Galileo. Desjardin says in a pamphlet entitled *Encore Galilée* (1877): "The Church has a sovran right to delay certain developments of science if she believes that in the existing circumstances they could be dangerous to the far higher interests of faith".[1] This at least is an outspoken admission of the logic of the ultramontane doctrine. Ehrhard, the liberal Catholic, does not go so far, but he tries to excuse the Roman Congregation in Galileo's case, on the ground that "its behaviour might have been morally less estimable if it had so easily abandoned the traditional interpretation of the Bible".[2]

(6) The method and principles, by which the old scholastic doctors pursued the study of theology, are at least in agreement with the needs of our time and the progress of science.

This startling statement was based on a letter of Pius IX. in 1862 to the Archbishop of Freising, in which he declared scholasticism to be the true Catholic method. It corresponds to the largely successful movement of the Jesuits to suppress all modern developments of Catholic theology and make

[1] *Encore Galilée*, pp. 50-51 (second edition). This is much more a paraphrase than an exceedingly free translation.

[2] Ehrhard, *Der Katholizismus u. das zwanzigste Jahrhundert*, p. 152.

the system of St. Thomas Aquinas authoritative. Pope Leo XIII., who had been brought up in the Jesuit Collegium Romanum, particularly favoured and furthered this policy. In little more than a year after he became Pope, in August 1879, he issued the Encyclical *Aeterni patris*, known as the Thomas-Encyclical, in which he raised St. Thomas, the prince of the scholastics, to the rank of patron of science and declared his works to be the supreme norm for the pursuit of all science and learning. In this curious document Leo XIII. says that all human science must hope for progress, and may expect a very considerable advance from a revival of philosophy on the lines of St. Thomas.[1]

Scholasticism is one of the chief planks in the ultramontane platform.

(7) Philosophy must not be studied independently of revelation.

In other words, philosophy must be the handmaid of theology.

This group of theses closes with the following note: "N.B. The errors of Anton Günther are mainly con-

[1] Cf. his brief of 1880: "We are convinced that the Thomist doctrine possesses, in a pre-eminent degree, a singular force and virtue to cure those evils by which our epoch is afflicted. We are of opinion that the time has arrived to add this new honour to the immortal glory of St. Thomas Aquinas. Here, then, is the chief motive which so determines us; it is because St. Thomas is the most perfect model in the divers branches of science that Catholics can take to themselves. . . . His doctrine is so vast that, like the sea, it embraces all that has come down to us from the ancients . . . because his doctrine, being composed of, and, as it were, armed by principles permitting of a great breadth of application, satisfies the necessities, not of one epoch only, but of all time; and because it is very efficacious in conquering those errors which are perpetually being reborn."

nected with the system of rationalism. They are condemned in papal letters, of 1857 to the Cardinal Archbishop of Cöln and of 1860 to the Bishop of Breslau."[1] Günther was a Catholic philosopher and theologian who died in 1863, who worked out a system of his own, and had a large circle of disciples.

The general object and effect, as you can see, of this paragraph of seven errors is not to reject reason or condemn science, but to render both reason and science the slaves, bound hand and foot, of ecclesiastical authority.

The next paragraph brings us to politics, although the subject concerned is religion. The principles implied are as follows:

(1) It is *not* lawful for the individual to accept and profess that religion which, guided by the light of reason, he considers true.

(2) Man cannot by practising any religion find the way of eternal salvation and reach eternal bliss.

(3) Good hopes cannot be entertained of the eternal happiness of all those who are not in the Church of Christ.

(4) Protestantism is not merely a different form of the same Christian faith, in which God can be pleased as well as in the Catholic Church.

Of course all these propositions are well known orthodox tenets of the Catholic Church. The significant point is that they should be introduced here. The Pope flings in the face of Europe those drastic tenets that either offend or amuse non-Catholics. But this is done in order to assert the unreserved

[1] Friedrich, ii. pp. 305-7.

opposition of the Church to the constitutions generally prevailing in Europe, which made freedom of conscience fundamental. The inwardness of the paragraph is this ecclesiastico-political bearing, and it forms a transition to the rest of the Encyclical.

The next paragraph does not state a number of particular erroneous theses. It enumerates generally a mixed group of condemnable errors and institutions. It runs thus:

Socialism, communism, secret societies, Bible societies, societies of liberal clergy: such pestilences are often and in the severest phrases condemned in Encyclicals of 1846, 1849 and 1863, and in Allocutions of 1849 and 1854.

What is common to these things is that they are pestilences in the eyes of ultramontanism. A reference to the documents shows that of the secret societies the principal one in view is Freemasonry, which it has always been the object of the Catholic Church to demolish. No Pope has been more active in combating Freemasonry than Leo XIII. In this Encyclical *Humanum genus* of April 1884 he marshalled all the documentary evidence he could discover against that black sect, and at the same time the Congregation of the Inquisition sent an elaborate instruction to the bishops and clergy as to the methods they should use to fight against Freemasonry. Another Encyclical in 1894 denounced the Freemason sect again, as an uncanny load pressing upon the Catholic nations. In a brief especially intended for Italy in 1892 he advised a method almost equivalent to boycotting persons suspected of belonging to the sect, for instance, doctors. It is delightfully humorous to find that when he himself became extremely ill in 1899, his horror of the pernicious society did not deter him from employing the Freemason surgeon Mazzoni to perform the necessary operation.

The bitter hostility of the Papacy to Freemasonry in the second half of the last century had, of course, its special cause in the part which the Freemasons played in bringing about the unity of Italy, and afterwards in determining the attitude of the Italian State towards the Church. The Jesuits and their organ, *Civiltà Catholica*, worked hard to stir up a general feeling of fear and aversion towards Freemasonry. They represented the Freemason Society as "spreading itself like an iron net over two hemispheres, and under the mask of progress and culture aiming at a general social revolution and the destruction of Christianity".

In the fifth paragraph, which includes 20 errors, we have the formal declaration of war on the Modern State. It is entitled "Errors concerning the Church and its Rights", and its most important theses are specified in the Encyclical *Quanta Cura*.

The Church is a true and perfect, entirely free society, and it preserves its own permanent rights conferred on it by its divine founder; and it is not the business of the State to determine what are the rights of the Church and within what limits it may exercise them.

This principle touches the centre of the controversies respecting the relation of the Church to the State. It asserts that the Church, as an independent society, is not bound to submit to the laws of the

State. It may be illustrated not only by the struggles on important questions, but by matters in which it might not be thought there would be any conflict. The Jesuit Wernz says: The Church is not obliged *vere et proprie* to observe the civil laws of the State passed for the public safety and sanitary reasons (respecting cemeteries), because they are State laws.[1] Other theses in the *Syllabus* are closely connected with the principle. The next is a logical corollary from it.

(2) The ecclesiastical power may exercise its authority without the permission and consent of the secular power.

(3) The Church has the power to decide dogmatically that the religion of the Catholic Church is the only true one.

This principle implies the doctrine that all baptized Christians, to whatever sect they belong, are subject to the jurisdiction of the Catholic Church, in contradistinction to Jews and heathen. If the Church cannot exercise that jurisdiction actually over heretics, and if the heretics themselves are quite unconscious of this obligation, the theory comes into force when a heretic is converted. Pius IX. applied the theory when he wrote to the Emperor William in 1873 that every baptized person belongs in some way to the Pope. The Emperor wrote back: "The Evangelical religion to which I, as your Holiness knows, belong, with my forefathers and the majority of my subjects, does not allow any mediator in our relationship with God, except Christ".[2]

[1] Cf. F. X. Wernz, *Jus decretale* (1901). There was a third edition in 1913.

[2] Nielsen, *History of the Papacy in the Nineteenth Century*, ii. p. 444.

(4) The obligation which binds Catholic teachers and writers is not confined to that which is prescribed as an article of belief by the infallible voice of the Church.

This thesis rather belongs to the context of the third paragraph, which concerns the attitude of the Church to science. How the ultramontanes interpret this principle in regard to history will be apparent from a couple of quotations from Catholic writers in Germany on the subject. One lays down the following precept: "A Catholic historian must consider it his strict duty to base his own historical view of the Reformation on the view held by the Church, which is alone right and therefore objective". Another writes: "The Catholic historian must take his standard for estimating events from the eternal objective principles of the Church as the *columna ac fundamentum veritatis*".[1]

(5) The Roman Popes and the general councils have not transcended the limits of their power; they have not usurped the rights of princes, or committed errors in defining matters of faith and morals.

In this thesis Pius IX. certainly did not intend to convey that no Pope had ever committed a mistake in his policy or actions. The object of the thesis is to defend the hierocratic system, as it was conducted by Popes and Councils in the Middle Ages, and to assert that the Popes who kept themselves within the limits of that system were not guilty of usurpation; for the system recognised the right to depose secular princes and abrogate secular laws. On July

[1] Hüffer.

21, 1871, Pius expressly declared to a deputation that "the Papal right to depose princes rests on temporal reasons, and as these do not exist now, the right is no longer used". It is hardly unfair to say that if they do not use it now, it is because they cannot; in theory they claim sovran authority over the world, governments as well as peoples. The right simply lies in abeyance.

(6) The Church has the power to employ external force; she also possesses a direct and an indirect temporal power (*potestas temporalis*).

This is one of the most important principles in ultramontane theory, and its declaration here was a considerable stumbling-block to Catholics who were not extreme. Even some of the ultramontane interpreters have tried to weaken its significance. The milder explanation is that it merely expresses the general theocratic doctrine of the indirect authority of the Church over the temporal sphere. We must look to the ultramontane explanation, which accords with the plain meaning of the words. Schrader in his commentary says significantly, "it is not merely the spirits of men that are subject to the power of the Church".[1] The most authoritative organ of the Roman Church, which was influential in promoting the publication of the *Syllabus*, the *Civiltà Catholica*, in 1853 described the Inquisition as a "sublime spectacle of social perfection". It is, in short, the ideal. The *Analecta Ecclesiastica*, a Roman journal, in 1895 exclaimed: "*O benedictas rogorum flammas*, O blessed flames of funeral pyres

[1] His "Vorwort". Cf. Acton, *History of Freedom*, p. 502.

by which, with the sacrifice of a few crafty wretches, hundreds of regiments of souls were saved! O glorious and venerable memory of Thomas Torquemada!"

Of course, prudence and policy dictate that this theory, which cannot at the present day be reduced to practice, should be kept in the background. Brors, in the little manual I have already mentioned—intended to diffuse ultramontane principles among German Catholics—has this passage on the Inquisition: "A heretic is a man who knowingly and against his conscience falls away from the true faith. That is a great sin, for which he deserves eternal punishment in hell. A heretic has also merited earthly punishment."[1] Liberal journalists discovered this sentence, and Brors had to try to explain it away. The attitude of the Society of Jesus may be found in the most recent official edition of their constitution, the *Institutum Societatis Jesu* (1869). There in the rules it is laid down that "pupils who attend the schools of the society shall not go to public spectacles, to see comedies or games, or to witness the execution of criminals, *nisi forte haereticorum*".[2] The most moderate expansion of the theory, in the Staatslexikon of the Görres Society by Schanz, runs: "The Church exercises jurisdiction over its subjects, and for this end must employ also external punishments, like any organised society".[3] This claim evidently includes everything that in this regard the ultramontane theory requires: it is simply the Inquisition.

[1] F. X. Brors, *Modernes A B C für Katholiken aller Hände*, § 131.
[2] ii. p. 114.
[3] Second ed., 1901-4.

In the next lecture I will continue the analysis of the *Syllabus*. It is indispensable to study it carefully for anyone who is interested in watching the behaviour of the Roman Catholic Church in the present age.

II

THE SYLLABUS

I PROCEED with the remainder of the fifth paragraph of the *Syllabus of Errors*, relating to the Church and its rights. You will remember that I convert the theses into the positive form which expresses the true doctrine.

(7) Besides the power which inheres in the Episcopate, the Episcopate does not possess another temporal power expressly or tacitly conceded to it by the State, and therefore capable of being revoked if the State wishes.

The point of this is that concessions made by the State cannot be revoked.

(8) The Church has an innate (*nativum*) and legal right to acquire and possess property.

This requires no special commentary; its fundamental importance is plain. It asserts the principle of the Dead Hand, and protests against the practice of modern States to limit the acquisition of Ecclesiastical property—as, *e.g.*, in Italy, France, and Germany.

(9) The consecrated servants of the Church, and the Roman Pontiff, are not to be excluded through-

out from all management and dominion of temporal things.

This touches, among other things, the question whether ecclesiastics as such should be ineligible as representatives in Parliament. It is one on which Catholic opinion seems to be divided.

(10) It is lawful for bishops without the permission of the civil government to publish Apostolic letters.

(11) Graces granted by the Roman Pontiff must not be considered invalid though they have not been asked for by the government.

These two theses repudiate the *placetum regium* which was required in Bavaria, Saxony, and other German Catholic States, as well as in France.

(12) The immunity of the Church and ecclesiastical persons is not derived from the civil law.

Immunity means freedom from secular jurisdiction, taxes, public burdens, and military service; and the point is that these principles are not revocable. Of course, no modern State recognises these principles, which are purely mediaeval.

(13) The jurisdiction of Ecclesiastical Courts (*Forum ecclesiasticum*) for clergy in secular cases, both civil and criminal, is not to be entirely abolished even without asking the Apostolic Chair or against its protestation.

In the Concordats, the Pope surrenders the *privilegium fori*, but this thesis expresses the theory which is still taught by the ultramontanes: the practical abandonment of the claim to ecclesiastical jurisdiction is due to the circumstances of the time.

(14) Without a violation of natural right and equity, the personal immunity of the clergy from military service cannot be abolished; civil progress does not demand such abolition, even in a State whose Constitution is liberal.

(15) It belongs exclusively to the ecclesiastical sphere of jurisdiction, by its own proper right, to direct theological studies.

This repudiates the claim of the State to exercise any supervision over theological seminaries and the education of candidates for the priesthood. It was a question that was to come up, as we shall see, in Bismarck's campaign against ultramontanism in 1873.[1]

(16) The doctrine which compares the Roman Pontiff to a free Prince exercising his sovranty in the universal Church is not a doctrine which came into prevalence in the Middle Ages.

On this Schrader observes: This doctrine "corresponds to the constitution of the Church and therefore must prevail in all ages".[2] It represents the dogmatical as opposed to the historical conception of the Papacy.

(17) There *are* reasons which forbid the transference of the Pontificate from the Roman Bishop and from the city of Rome to another bishop and another city, whether by the decree of a general council or by the act of all the peoples (*universorum populorum facto*).

[1] Cf. K. von Schlözer (uncle), *Römische Briefe,* and K. von Schlözer (nephew), *Letzte römische Briefe.* They set forth Bismarck's relations with the Vatican. Goyau, *Bismarck et l'Église,* 4 vols., are useful.

[2] P. 61.

The reason, of course, is the doctrine of the Primacy alleged to have been entrusted to Peter by the Founder of Christianity. It is enough to say that the doctrine has been affirmed by the authority of the Vatican Council.

(18) The decision of a national council admits of further discussion (*i.e.* it is not final) and the civil government cannot appeal to this decision.

[*I.e.* the assent of the Pope is necessary.]

(19) No national Churches can be instituted which are withdrawn from the authority of the Roman Pontiff and completely separated.

(20) Excessively arbitrary acts on the part of the Roman Pontiff have not contributed to the schism of the Eastern and Western Churches.

This thesis, of course, has only significance as a canon fettering the judgments of Catholic historians.

The most numerous and most important parts of this paragraph, of which I have reproduced the contents, concern the relation of the Church to the State. The next paragraph covers a good deal of the same ground but from the other side, from the point of view of the State. It is entitled "Errors concerning civil society both in itself and in its relation to the Church", and contains 17 theses. It is intimately connected with the preceding.

(1) The State (*status respublicae*) does not possess, as origin and source of all rights, an unlimited right.

Taken abstractly this proposition may command wide assent. The Jesuit Riess has paraphrased it as follows: "If some rights have their source in the

State, it is not the origin of *right in general*, which is rather to be sought in God, by whom rights can be granted independently of the State".[1] This *right in general* is, of course, the right of the Church. In a manifesto addressed to the Prussian Ministry by the Prussian Roman Catholic bishops in 1873 on the promulgation of the anti-clerical laws, they wrote thus: "The Church cannot admit the principle of the Luther State that the laws of the State are the ultimate source of all right, and that the Church possesses only those rights which the Legislature and Constitution of the State grant it, without denying the divinity of Christ and the divine nature of His doctrine and institution, without making Christianity itself depend on the arbitrary will of men". As a matter of fact, both this declaration and the *Syllabus* ascribe to the State a claim which is not usually made for it.

(2) The doctrine of the Catholic Church is not contrary to the prosperity and weal of human society.

(3) The government of the State has not an indirect negative power in religious matters, and the less so if it is exercised by an unbelieving prince; thus it has neither the right of *exequatur*, nor the right of appeal which is known as *ab abusu*.

The denial of the right of *exequatur* is a repetition of the denial of the *placetum regium* in a previous thesis, and concerns the legislative and adminis-

[1] Florian Riess, *Die moderne Irrlehre oder Liberalismus*, p. 39. It is to be found in that convenient collection, "Stimmen aus Maria-Laach", which comments on different aspects of the Encyclical of December 8, 1864.

trative activity of the Church. The appeal *ab abusu* is the limit imposed by the State on the Church's judicial activity. It existed in France under the old régime, and it exists in the Catholic German States to-day. It was introduced into Prussia in 1873 and abolished in 1886: Bismarck described its effect as striking water with a sword.

(4) In case of a conflict between the laws of the two powers, the civil power is not the superior.

This is one of the most often cited principles of the *Syllabus*, and is fundamental in Papal doctrine.[1]

(5) The civil power has not the right to limit, to interpret, or to abolish solemn conventions (commonly called Concordats) concluded with the Holy See concerning the exercise of rights pertaining to ecclesiastical immunities, without the consent of the Holy See, or in the face of its protests.

This repeats in another form a principle laid down in a former thesis. It had a historical motive in an event of 1860. A Concordat had been concluded with Baden in 1859. In 1860 Baden annulled it, superseding it by a State law. The Pope desisted from his opposition when the government stood firm. We have a recent example in the Separation Law in France, which annulled the Concordats of 1801.

The strict ultramontane theory of the Concordats is one-sided, and this is a natural consequence of

[1] Cf. Cardinal Lépicier, *De Stabilitate et Progressu Dogmatis* (1910), pp. 193-217, and especially the Appendix, for a modern statement of this position. He dwells upon the right of the Church to constrain heretics, whether members or non-members of the Church. Pius X. expressly approved of this book, and published a letter expressing his approval.

their principles. They consider the Concordat as a privilege which the Pope grants and can revoke when it pleases him; while on the other hand the State has no right to withdraw. But practically they do not press this logic, and they regard the Concordat as a contract.

(6) The civil power can *not* interfere in matters of religion, morality, and ecclesiastical government. Hence it cannot judge concerning the instructions which the pastors of the Church issue by virtue of their office to guide consciences; nor can it decide concerning the ministration of the divine sacraments and the dispositions necessary to receive them.

Observe that in the last clause the *sacramenta* include marriage: on that subject more is said. This thesis repeats the repudiation of supervision or interference by the State, already laid down in previous theses of this paragraph, and implied elsewhere; but it goes further and applies the principle to the field of morals, as if the State had no right to interfere in matters of morals, except under the direction of the Church. Catholic writers have been at some pains to weaken or soften the meaning; but the principle is part of the logical system of ultramontanism.

The next four theses are of great importance, because they embody the Papal theory of education, the gravest question nowadays on which Church and State come into sharp collision.

(7) It is not true that the whole management of public schools, in which the youth of a Christian State is educated, with the exception only in a

qualified way of episcopal seminaries, can and ought to be assigned to the civil authority in such a way that no other authority should be recognised as having a right to interfere in the school discipline, in the arrangement of the studies, in the granting of degrees, and in the choice and approval of teachers.

(8) *A fortiori* the method of studies in the clerical seminaries is not subject to State supervision.

(9) The best social-political system does not require that the popular schools which are open to children of all classes, and in general the public institutions which are intended for the higher instruction and education of youth, should be removed from all authority, management and interference on the part of the Church and submitted fully to the will of the civil and political authority, so as to be guided by the views of the government and the common opinion of the age.

(10) Catholics cannot approve of a kind of education which quite ignores the Catholic faith and the authority of the Church, and which regards exclusively, or at least as the chief aim, only the knowledge of nature and the ends of secular (earthly) society.

In this theory of education two points are to be observed. In the first place, though it is not referred to here, you will find in orthodox Catholic expositions that the principle on which the objection to compulsory State education is based is that the education of children is the indefeasible right of the parents and the parents alone. But the Church is the universal educational institution established by God; and the parents therefore stand in their educational function under the guiding influence of the

Church. Hence the parents have not the position of sovran power in respect of the Church, but are merely organs of the Church. Thus the parental right is insisted on merely to hand it over to the Church.

In the second place, education is inseparable from instruction. The Church insists on control of instruction in secular subjects, choice of teachers, etc.

This is theory. In practical politics, what the Catholics strive for is to have, besides the State schools, free schools of their own exclusively under clerical guidance, which means an ultramontane education.

(11) The State has no right to hinder the bishops and the faithful from freely communicating with the Roman See.

At the present day there are virtually no hindrances in any State.

(12) The secular government has not of itself the right to present bishops and cannot require them to enter upon the administration of their dioceses before they receive from the Pope canonical institution in the Apostolic letter.

(13) And the State has not the right to depose bishops from the exercise of their pastoral office, and it has the obligation to obey the Roman Bishop in what concerns the Episcopate and the institution of bishops.

We have an instance of the violation of this principle in the deposition (and imprisonment) of Cardinal Ledochowski, Archbishop of Gnesen and Posen, by the Prussian Government in 1874.

The next two theses concern religious orders.

(14) The State cannot by its own right change the age prescribed by the Church for taking religious vows by men or women, nor forbid all religious orders to allow any one to take such vows without permission of the government.

(15) Those laws should not be abolished which concern the protection of religious orders, their rights and duties; further, the secular power cannot afford its support to all who wish to desert the religious order they have entered and break their solemn vows; nor can it utterly abolish such religious societies or collegiate churches or simple benefices even if they be under the right of patronage, or submit and consign their property and revenues to secular administration and disposal.

These theses are directed against the laws which most States found it necessary to pass. Recent French history is an eloquent comment.

The last two theses of this paragraph are of a general and sweeping kind.

(16) Kings and princes are not exempt from the jurisdiction of the Church; and in the decision of questions of jurisdiction they are not superior to the Church.

This is, of course, already implied in the general theory of ecclesiastical supremacy. Schrader's comment is: "Princes should remember that their power is entrusted to them not merely to rule the world, but chiefly to protect the Church".

(17) The Church is not to be separated from the State, nor the State from the Church.

This is the mediaeval theory, by which the Church was the State, the only sovran State in the full sense. Catholics accept separation only as a lesser evil.

Recently, in regard to the Separation question in France, this thesis of the *Syllabus* was appealed to by the organ of the Vatican, the *Osservatore romano*, in (August) 1904.

We now pass to the seventh paragraph, containing 9 theses, on Errors relating to natural and Christian ethics. The first two concern the basis of rationalistic ethics; the second two deal with the special doctrine of materialism; the rest treat of practical consequences of such views for society.

(1) Moral laws require divine sanction, and it is at least necessary that human laws should be made consistent with natural law, or should receive their binding force from God.

(2) The science of philosophy and ethics, and the civil laws, shall not and ought not to deviate from divine revelation and the authority of the Church.

I may quote a passage from the little manual of Brors (already referred to) which will illustrate the practical consequences deducible from these principles: "The Church has the power to declare null and void those ordinances of the State which injure the moral and religious interest of men. The Church must take care that her subjects do not suffer spiritual hurt by the ordinances of the secular power."[1]

(3) Other forces must be recognised besides those which reside in *matter*, and all moral discipline and goodness ought not to be placed in accumulating

[1] Cf. *Modernes A B C für Katholiker aller Hände*, § 131.

and increasing riches by every means and enjoying pleasures.

(4) Right (*jus*) does not consist in material fact, nor are all duties an empty name, nor have all human deeds a valid right (*via iuris*).

(5) Authority is something different from numbers and the sum of material forces.

The point of this is to denounce the sovranty of the people and democracy as resting on a purely materialistic basis. It is, however, rather awkward that many Jesuit theologians have maintained the theory of popular sovranty. And as a matter of fact the Centre in the German Reichstag are supporters of universal suffrage.

The next two theses touch the question of *faits accomplis*, that we saw was treated in the Encyclical *Quanta Cura*.

(6) A successful injustice is detrimental to the sanctity of right.

The application, of course, is the loss of the Papal States.

(7) The so-called principle of non-intervention is not to be proclaimed or observed.

As this principle that has come to be recognised as fundamental in modern international law secured the Italiancy of the Papal territory and afterwards the abolition of the temporal state entirely, and as it stood in the way of Papal hopes of recovering the temporal power, it was of crucial importance to the Pope. We shall meet the question again in 1871.

(8) It is not allowed to refuse obedience to legitimate princes nor to rise against them.

This has not such importance now; in the ultramontane theory it has to be qualified by the consideration how far the prince's power is legitimate, *i.e.* how far it does not contradict the will of God, interpreted by the Church.

(9) The violation of the most holy oaths and all criminal actions are not to be approved of, and are absolutely unlawful, when done from a patriotic motive.

The next paragraph contains ten errors on the theory of Christian marriage. I will not quote all the theses in full, but only what is of most importance.

If according to natural law the marriage bond is not indissoluble, yet in various cases divorce proper cannot lawfully be granted by the secular authority.

The Church has the power of laying down impediments to marriage, and therein she uses her own right, and not a right committed to her by the State.

The form of marriage laid down by the Council of Trent is obligatory, on penalty of the marriage not being valid, even when the secular law prescribes another form and makes validity dependent thereon.

True marriage of Christians cannot exist by a mere civil contract.

Matrimonial matters do not naturally belong to a secular court.

The sum of all this is the theory that marriage exclusively concerns the Church, and the State should have nothing to do with it—exactly like education. In both questions the ecclesiastical ideal and the principles of the modern State are diametrically opposed. It is important to observe that this is the ultramontane ideal, not by any means admitted by all Catholics in such an uncompromising form. The Catholic Martin, in his work on *Der Simultanstaat*,[1] recognises the necessity of the secular principle. Here is what he says: The extremists (*i.e.* the ultramontanes) "mistake completely the nature and features of the State, in thinking that civil marriage is a mere frivolous experiment of anticlerical liberalism, aiming at de-Christianising the State and destroying religion. If a State in the interest of religious freedom refuses to make ecclesiastical observances compulsory, or to visit the neglect of them by civil disadvantages, and if it declines to favour the ecclesiastical organisation of our confession above those of others, hardly any course remains for it but to prescribe a definite form of marriage and to leave to the individuals to fulfil the ecclesiastical obligations if they choose."

The paragraph is followed by a note: "Here may be mentioned two other errors concerning the abolition of the celibacy of the clergy, and concerning the superiority of the state of matrimony to that of celibacy; these errors are stabbed to the heart (*confodiuntur*), the first in the Encyclical of November 1846, the second in the Apostolic letter of June 1851".

[1] 1892, Bremen, 4 vols. Bury gives this information. On the other hand, the officials of the British Museum, the Bodleian, and the London Library cannot trace this book. Bungeroth wrote *Der Simultanstaat* (Bremen, 1892–93), but I searched his four volumes in vain for any quotation even distantly resembling the above.

The next paragraph consists of 2 theses on the temporal power of the Pope.

(1) The sons of the Christian and Catholic Church are *not* divided in opinion as to the compatibility of the temporal sovranty with the spiritual.

(2) The abolition of the temporal sovranty which the Apostolic Chair possesses would not contribute in a high degree to freedom and the happiness of the Church.

Then follows a note: "Besides these errors explicitly censured, several are implicitly reproved, by the assertion of the doctrine which all Catholics most firmly hold, as to the temporal sovranty". (The allocutions and letters are cited in which the doctrine is set forth.)

The last paragraph of the *Syllabus* denounces four errors of modern Liberalism, and maintains the following principles:

(1) It is still expedient in our days that the Catholic religion should be treated as the only religion of the State, to the exclusion of all other worship whatsoever.

(2) It was therefore not a good thing that in certain Catholic countries the free exercise of their worship was guaranteed by law to persons settling in them.

(3) For it is not false to say that the freedom granted by the State to every worship and the permission to all to profess openly all kinds of opinion and views lead to the corruption of the morals and minds of the peoples and to the propagation of the pestilence of indifferentism.

These three theses form an argument: The first

lays down the general principle of intolerance, the second condones its practical application, the third brings forward a reason for its adoption. They represent the orthodox ultramontane theory of intolerance; but in countries where Catholics are in a minority and it is their policy to appear tolerant, the ultramontanes have sought to migitate the doctrine by all sorts of subtle interpretations. The practical principle applied, of course, is to denounce toleration of Protestantism in Catholic lands, with an appeal to the ultramontane doctrine, but to claim toleration of Catholicism in Protestant lands, with an appeal to the modern doctrine of toleration. But theoretically, as the *Syllabus* and the Encyclical *Quanta Cura* lay down, toleration is unreservedly false, and if the Catholics had the power in the world no toleration would be defensible. There is an emotional expression often cited of the abhorrence of toleration in the work of Roh, a German ultramontane, entitled *Die Grundirrthümer unserer Zeit*. "Tolerance!" he exclaims contemptuously, "fair word for superficial people, and the highest that three and a half centuries could produce! . . . We use the word *tolerate* of something which ought not to exist and we should like to abolish. For instance, every animal tolerates parasites, who pay for their lodging by pricking and biting. . . . Whenever the word *tolerance* is used, I feel a chill in my heart. It hides hate and bitterness! Away with Toleration! But, O divine charity, remain always with us."[1] The inquisitors considered their work as *charity*.

[1] P. Roh, *Die Grundirrthümer unserer Zeit*, pp. 61-2.

We now reach the last thesis of this paragraph and of the *Syllabus* itself.

(4) The Roman pontiff cannot, and ought not to, reconcile himself and come to terms with progress, liberalism, and modern civilisation.

This drastic declaration is the more impressive, coming as the finish of the document. It is a perfectly logical consequence of the whole theory, perfectly in accordance with the spirit of the doctrine of the *Syllabus* and the *Encyclical*, which are uncompromisingly mediaeval. In interpreting the thesis, the ultramontanes distinguish between true and false civilisation, true and false progress, and say that the Church is not opposed to true civilisation. This distinction does not take us any further; for their true civilisation means that which corresponds to the doctrine of the Roman Church, *i.e.* mediaevalism, and so the question is merely a verbal one. Leo XIII. saw in the opinions, views, laws, and life of contemporary society a retrogression to heathendom. His Encyclical *Libertas* of June 1888 is a condemnation of liberalism as immoral. It has been called the classical heresy of the nineteenth century.

The *Syllabus* and the *Encyclical* were welcomed with enthusiasm by the ultramontanes, and with malicious joy by freethinkers and Protestants. To Liberal Catholics it was a painful blow, as it was intended to be. The Bishop of Orleans, Dupanloup, stepped into the breach,[1] and published a pamphlet

[1] Acton, *Zur Geschichte des Vatikan-Konzils*, p. 3; Friedrich, *Geschichte des Vatikan-Konzils*, i. pp. 649 ff., ii. p. 374. Many of the French bishops, and even Dupanloup, were under the delusion that a Council would curb intemperate zeal.

on "The September Convention and the Encyclical", which created a great stir.[1] It was a clever tactical device to unite the Roman question on which he took the offensive, with the *Syllabus* on which he maintained the defensive. He defended it by means of theological distinctions and definitions, seeking to show that the Pope did not really condemn freedom and progress. Comparing the documents on which the *Syllabus* was based, he tried to point out that misunderstandings arose when they were taken out of the context. But it was the Pope who had taken them out of the context. Then he elaborated the proposition that such terms as liberty, liberalism, progress, civilisation are ambiguous; and that these things were condemned only in certain extreme senses.

The Pope had been rather alarmed at the sensation created by his pronouncements, evoking cries of hatred and defiance. In Belgium especially, where the whole political system rested on freedom of worship, there was consternation, and in February 1865 the *Civiltà Catholica* found it necessary to assure the Belgians that the *Syllabus* and *Encyclical* did not attack the Belgian constitution nor touch the rights, duties, and political liberties of Belgian citizens. In France, the government on January 1 forbade the bishops to publish the documents till further notice, as containing matter opposed to the constitution of the Empire; and a few days later this prohibition was withdrawn, except as regards the first part of the *Encyclical*. Some of the prelates were recalcitrant, and read the forbidden part, for which an action was brought against them.

[1] Lagrange, *Vie de Mgr. Dupanloup*, iii. p. 90.

In the circumstances, the pamphlet of the Bishop of Orleans toning down the Papal meaning was not unwelcome to the Pope, and he received a letter (February 4) officially acknowledging it in terms which seemed to be approbative. But afterwards the Pope approved of Schrader's commentary on the *Syllabus*, which was absolutely different from that of the Liberal Catholic. The ultramontanes repudiated and censured Dupanloup's interpretation, which they called the Anti-Syllabus, and described as "violating the teaching of the Holy See so far as to make it mean what it really condemns". "The Encyclical", said the writer of the *Univers*, "would have united all Catholics; the Bishop of Orleans has made everything doubtful. . . . My opinion is that the Bishop is courting the Tuileries."[1]

How is it that two such different interpretations as that of the Liberal Catholic Dupanloup and the ultramontane Schrader could be alike accepted by the Vatican? How is it that ultramontanes themselves, when they choose, can explain away what seems the plain and obvious meaning of the *Syllabus*, and accept principles to which it seems to be opposed? The answer lies in the distinction between *thesis* and *hypothesis*. The *Syllabus* is concerned with *thesis*, the laying down of principles, which are of absolute validity, and would prevail in an ideal society when the Church possessed the power of enforcing its authority, as it did to such a vast extent in the Middle Ages. But in modern times the Church in

[1] D'Ideville, *Journal d'un diplomat en Italie*, pp. 282 f. Bury paraphrases the last sentence; it is not a translation. Cf. Séché, *Les Derniers Jansénistes*, iii. pp. 200 f.

practice has to deal with *hypothesis*, *i.e.* it has to determine its actions to meet certain given conditions which it cannot control; it has to compromise and conciliate its theoretical principles, up to a certain point, with actual circumstances. This it has had to do in the interests of self-preservation; the Concordat of 1801 began the policy. But notwithstanding this unwilling and necessary condescension, the Papacy never abandoned the theoretical principles which are the logical consequence of its claim to independent sovran authority, superior to the civil authority; they remain in the background as the ideal, like a utopia, which the Church would realise if it could. On the other hand, the Pope had no illusions that there was any chance of realising them at present. Thus the ultramontane interpretation of the *Syllabus* as thesis was perfectly correct; on the other hand, the softer interpretation of the French Liberal Catholic was, though not literally sound, yet in spirit at least *just*, in so far as it went to show that there was no practical danger that the Papacy would not continue to compromise and find, however reluctantly, a *modus vivendi* with modern political institutions.

What, it may be asked, was the purpose or use of publishing and advertising the theory, which modern society was beginning to forget, and accentuating the fundamental antagonism between the Church and the modern State in such a way as to excite and aggravate the suspiciousness with which the Church was regarded by statesmen? The explanation of this, I believe, lies in the spread of liberal ideas among bishops and clergy in France and

Germany. The *Syllabus* was a blow aimed at liberal Catholicism; it was intended to crush the *thesis* of Liberal Catholics that liberalism and modern constitutional liberties were good in themselves. To ultramontanism, in playing its long game, this is a matter of supreme importance. The first and essential condition of ever attaining to a partial realisation of its ideal is to ultramontanism the Catholic world; and here its foe was and is liberal Catholicism. Hence the *Syllabus* is far from being a dead document of mere historical interest. It is still alive, and forms one of the main foundations and sources of the ultramontane literature of the present day. In 1903 the Cardinal Archbishop Fischer of Cöln said in his pastoral letter to his clergy: "The Syllabus of Errors is a touchstone of our own time; by which we can decide what agrees with Catholic truth and what contradicts it. It is to be regretted that recently some Catholic writers have ventured, in order to sustain their own opinions, to lessen or set aside the force and authority of this important document." The reference is to the writers of the new Catholic reform movement in Germany.

Thus it is equally important for the Papacy, in pursuance of its aims, to propagate the true theoretical doctrine regarding the relations between Church and State among Catholics, that is the *thesis*, while in its dealings with governments and its public policy it acts on the *hypothesis*. Its ideal is supremacy; what it claims is freedom. Bismarck in 1884 (November 26) in the Reichstag thus addressed the Centre: "You are fighting, you say, for the freedom of the Church! What do you mean by freedom of the Church? You really mean the rule of the Church. As soon as your rule is endangered, you talk of a Diocletian persecution, slavery and oppression; ruling is born in your bones from old traditions."[1] This is rhetorical, but it contains the truth that the kind of freedom which is claimed on the plea of liberal principles is a step to the domination which is claimed on ecclesiastical principles.

I may say a word more on the ecclesiastical theory of history which is implied as we saw in some of the theses of the *Syllabus*. One of the features of the ultramontane view is that it refuses to distinguish between historical periods. It will not recognise that the early Church of the Graeco-Roman world was different from the Church of the Middle Ages, and that the modern Church must be different from the mediaeval. This unhistorical view is necessitated by the adhesion to the secular pretensions of the mediaeval Church; which pretensions in turn have to be made good by the alleged theory and practice of the early Church. Further, the history of European civilisation is judged according as in a particular period it was or was not under the guidance of the Roman Church. This way of looking at things is a fundamental point of opposition between the Church and modern thought. No conciliation is possible between the dogmatic point of view and the historical principle, which is one of the most important acquisitions of the nineteenth century. Cardinal

[1] Cf. *Briefe Bismarcks an Leop. v. Gerlach*, pp. 121-4; Busch, *Our Chancellor*, i. p. 158. The quotation is in Bismarck, *Politische Reden*, x. (1894) p. 259. The new edition of Bismarck's *Werken* has not yet reached 1884.

Manning felt this when he said that the dogma must conquer history.[1]

[1] Fénelon argues similarly, for he holds that the Church is supreme over fact as over doctrine. Is she not the supreme expounder of tradition, which is a chain of facts? Fénelon writes: "Oserait-on soutenir que l'Église après avoir mal raisonné sur tous les textes, et les avoir pris à contre-sens, est tout à coup saisie par un enthousiasme aveugle, pour juger bien, en raisonnant mal?" Bury recurred to this *obiter dictum* in his *Ancient Greek Historians*, p. 238: "This was the first appearance of the principle which Cardinal Manning expressed . . . in his famous saying that dogma must overcome history, and which guides all the historiography of the Ultramontane school". Dupanloup held, "surtout, méfiez-vous des sources". Cf. Manning, *The Temporal Mission of the Holy Ghost*, pp. 202-3; his *Pastoral on the Infallibility of the Roman Pontiff*, p. 126. Above all, cf. Quirinus, *Letters from Rome*, pp. 69, 348, 443. On p. 69 we read: "The dogma has triumphed over history, as Manning has so admirably explained in his last Pastoral". On p. 443 we read: "To quote a significant phrase in constant use here during this winter, 'the dogma must conquer history'." The footnote connects this phrase with Manning.

III

THE VATICAN COUNCIL

WE now come to the final act which completed and crowned the programme of ultramontanism, carried out in the pontificate of Pius IX.[1] I have already pointed out that the definition of the Immaculate Conception in 1854, the issue of the *Syllabus* in 1864, and the definition of Infallibility in 1870 are connected by a close logical interdependence; and though circumstances determined the time and mode of action, the various parts of the scheme were all contemplated in the early period of the pontificate.[2] I showed that the design of issuing a *Syllabus* of modern errors dated from the first years of Pius. I will now show more particularly the connexion of Infallibility with the Immaculate Conception.

In 1848 the French ultramontane party had announced a programme of which the four chief points were to procure (1) the promulgation of the Immaculate Conception, (2) the universal adoption of the Roman liturgy, (3) the canonisation of Bellar-

[1] Cf. Bury in the *R.P.A.* (1917). "The outstanding figure of the nineteenth century was to be, not Pius the Ninth, but Darwin" (p. 26). Cf. also Mourret, *Le Councile du Vatican*, p. 3.

[2] De la Gorce's chapter on the Vatican Council in his *Histoire du Second Empire*, vol. vi., is exceedingly imperfect.

mine as the father of ultramontanism, and (4) the definition of the personal infallibility of the Pope. Pius IX. had already, in the *Encyclical* of November 9, 1846—of which more than 10,000 copies were distributed—declared his infallibility in faith and morals, and in the same letter he had called Mary *immaculata.* In his exile at Gaeta he determined to raise the Immaculate Conception into a dogma, and on his return to Rome he began to work for that purpose with the ardent co-operation of the Jesuits, who had always set special store by this doctrine.[1] At Granada in the year 1588 some Jesuits had discovered a coffer containing tablets of lead and a parchment which among others furnished apostolic evidence for the Immaculate Conception. It was promptly shown by learned Dominicans that this testimony was a forgery.[2] And Urban VIII. in 1639 forbade any appeal to be made to the Tablets of Granada, and in 1682 Innocent XI. pronounced them forgeries and put them on the Index.[3] As to the doctrine itself, the Popes allowed it to remain open; but it spread greatly in Spain and Italy, and much pressure was put on Gregory XVI. to adopt it. Pius IX. first of all consulted the bishops;[4] the majority of replies was favourable to his project, and then he appointed a commission of theologians, including Perrone and Schrader,[5] to consider whether

[1] *Regensburger Zeitschrift,* "Das alkumenische Konzil vom Jahre 1869", i. p. 225.

[2] Preuss, *Die römische Lehre,* pp. 118 ff.; Döllinger, *Akad. Vorträge,* i. p. 249.

[3] Reusch, *Index,* ii. pp. 245 ff.

[4] Cecconi, *Storia del Concilio ecumenico Vaticano,* i. pp. 68 ff.

[5] *Ibid.* i. p. 80. On the members of the different commissions cf. Granderath, *Histoire du Concile du Vatican,* vol. i. pp. 92-6.

a dogma could be defined on the basis of tradition alone, without the testimony of Scripture. The commission decided that tradition was sufficient, and that tradition was proved if in various ages a number of witnesses can be produced. Then in November 1854 about 140 bishops came to Rome. Meetings were held in the Vatican; the Pope intimated that he was pleased at their presence at the definition of the new dogma. But let them not for a moment imagine they were a council, or express any opinion as to the opportuneness of the promulgation. The matter entirely rested with the Pope. The Bull was then read aloud, and they were invited to make remarks.[1] They criticised some of the daring assertions which it contained as to early evidence for the doctrine; some suggested that the wishes of the bishops should be mentioned; but this was met by the reply that the action of the Pope in making the decision alone revealed the infallibility with which Christ had invested his Vicar. The dogma was proclaimed in St. Peter's on December 8, 1854.

The event was of great importance, not of course on account of the nature of dogma itself, but on account of the method of its adoption by the Church.[2] It was a clear and unmistakable assertion of the infallibility and absolute sovranty of the Pope. He arrogated the right of making a new dogma an article of faith by his own sole authority, and his claim was not opposed except by isolated protests.

[1] The Bull Ineffabilis Deus is printed in *Lettres apostoliques de Pie IX*, p. 124.

[2] Nielsen, *History of the Papacy in the Nineteenth Century*, ii. pp. 195-6; Baunard, *Cardinal Pie*, ii. p. 401; Friedrich, *Tagebuch*, p. 294; Granderath, ii. pp. 295-9.

The general of the Dominican Order had been won over to the doctrine before the accession of Pius, and care had been taken to silence the opposition of that order, which, however, was no longer influential. The presence of the bishops on the occasion of the proclamation was a triumph of the Papal authority over the episcopate. The novelty of the act is fully acknowledged by the Jesuit Schrader in his work dealing with the *Syllabus*. "It is", he says, "an act to which no former pontificate can show a parallel; for the Pope defined the dogma of his own sovran authority, without the co-operation of a council; and this independent action involves practically, if not formally, another dogmatic definition, namely that the Pope is infallible in matters of faith in his own person and not merely when presiding at a council. The act of December 8, 1854, virtually claimed infallibility for the Pope."[1] It is also not unimportant to note that in both aspects the act was a great triumph for the Jesuits, and inaugurated the predominating influence they possessed throughout this pontificate. They had been always, like their founder, impassioned upholders of the doctrine; and henceforward they were to commemorate every year the heart of the Immaculate Mary with masses or fasts.

The Encyclical of 1846 to which I referred above declared, as the proclamation of the Immaculate dogma *implied*, the principle of Infallibility; but before proclaiming that principle itself, it was

[1] *Pius IX als Papst u. als König*, p. 12. Accompanying this work is "ein päpstliches Belobungschreiben". Cf. Friedrich, *Geschichte des vatikanischen Konzils*, i. pp. 345-6, 426-8.

thought necessary to make preparations which involved considerable delay, in order to invest it with a semblance of legality. A systematic agitation for this end was carried on; the revival of scholasticism and the issue of the *Syllabus* were important steps in the advance to the Vatican Council.

It is also to be observed that the definition of the Immaculate Conception not only assured Infallibility, but also, and just for that reason, rendered it necessary in the eyes of Pius to define it.[1] Until it had been formally defined as an article of faith, and set above all doubt, there was always the possibility that after his death his act might come to be considered a usurpation. This was a haunting nightmare which may have had a considerable effect in urging Pius along the path on which the Jesuits guided him.

I may digress here to call attention to certain psychological traits in Pius IX. which predisposed him to co-operate vigorously in a development which was mainly guided by the Jesuits and extreme ultramontanists.[2] He was exceedingly superstitious, in the common sense of the term, and credulous of legends and prophecies. In his youth, as Count Mastai, he had been cured of epilepsy by "water of Jesus of Nazareth" which was given him by a well-known prophetess of the day, Elizabeth Canori-Mora. Later, a more celebrated woman, Anna Maria Taigi, who was a great power in Rome, exercising

[1] Friedrich, *Tagebuch*, p. 294.

[2] Ollivier, in his *L'Empire libéral*, sketches the character of Pius IX. with power and pregnancy. The Pascal story, for instance, is really illuminating.

influence over cardinals and prelates, honoured successively by Pius VII., Leo XII., and especially by Gregory XV., was known to Pius, and she foretold his pontificate and the definition of Infallibility. As Pope, he often spoke of her prophecies, and he raised her memory to the ecclesiastical rank of "honourable" in 1863. Rosa Columba Asdente also prophesied his pontificate, and Marie Lataste foretold the definition of the Immaculate Conception. Leonardo of Porto Maurigio was canonised by Pius; in his tomb were found parchments with prophecies, of which one prognosticated the Immaculate Conception and declared it would abolish heresies and bring peace to the Church. In 1858 at Lourdes the Mother of God appeared and made a statement which to a profane ear seems meaningless: "I am the Immaculate Conception".[1] Pius favoured the Lourdes cult;[2] in 1876 he had the image crowned, and the bishops who were present referred to the epiphany of 1858 as confirming the proclamation of 1852.

In 1846 the Virgin appeared to two children at La Salette. She gave each of them a secret communication for Pius. He was very anxious to receive them and they reached him in 1851. He was highly pleased, but did not communicate the secrets to anyone. The message of Melania, however, apparently contained a prediction of the definition of Infallibility, for in writing the secret which was to be transmitted to Rome she asked how to spell Infallibility and antichrist. Missionaries soon settled

[1] Nielsen, ii. p. 197.

[2] Cf. Lafond, pp. 11, 91; Ollivier, ii. p. 324; Baunard, *Cardinal Pie*, ii. p. 401.

at La Salette; it became a place of pilgrimage and miracles; and the "Annales de Notre Dame de la Salette" were founded, to publish the wonder that occurred.

It is not an insignificant fact, in illustration of the Pope's mentality, that the letter containing Melania's secret reached the Pope's hands on July 18, 1851, and the dogma of Infallibility was declared on July 18, 1870. Archbishop Manning asserted that the Pope himself was not anxious for the definition of Infallibility; it mattered little to him, and he only acquiesced in the wishes of the Catholic world. This is simply false. Pius disavowed Manning's history of the Council, and sealed with his approval the history of Plantier. From it we learn that Pius recognised from the very beginning that Infallibility was to be one of the glorious tasks of his reign, and, convinced of this, he allowed nothing to deter him from carrying through the Council. He believed he had a special mission, and here we touch upon the point of contact between the Vatican Council and the miracles of La Salette. The destinies of the Church were affected by the visions and prophecies of neurotic women.

There grew up also something resembling a cult of the Pope himself, which was not surprising considering what he claimed to be. His claims were sometimes expressed by himself in a form which, if he were not a Pope, we should describe as megalomania.[1] He said in 1866, "I am the way, the truth

[1] Roman Catholic opposition in its various forms, learned in Germany, national in Italy, and liberal in France, was directed steadily against the Pope's claims.

and the life".[1] The *Civiltà Catholica* said about the same time, "When he meditates, it is God who thinks in him", and compared the mystery of his vicariate to the mystery of the sacrament—an analogy of which you can easily see the implication.

As that paper, the *Civiltà*, played an important rôle in the years immediately preceding the Vatican Council, it is necessary to point out, firstly, that it was edited by Jesuits, and secondly, that in February 1866 the Pope issued a Brief elevating it into something of the nature of a congregation. By this arrangement, the *Magister Palatini* reads the proofs and underlines passages, which are then erased in the Segretaria di Stato. Thus the paper authentically expresses the Papal ideas. But the Jesuits who act as editors are separated in a certain way from the order and are under the Pope's direct guidance. In this way the Society and the General are not responsible for the doctrines of the *Civiltà*, and in any country where the ultramontane principles inflexibly applied in that organ create offence or embarrassment, the order truthfully can say that it has nothing to do with the journal. But the editors belong to the order and are imbued with its true spirit, though they are responsible only to the Pope; and their independence of their order enables them to guide the Vatican far more effectually than if they received their directions from the General. Another paper, the *Correspondance di Roma* was founded and supported by Papal funds. The power of journal-

[1] Lord Acton and Bury both believed Pius IX. to have made this amazing outburst, but I am not certain that he did make it.

ism was now recognised at Rome, and was actively used for preparing the way for Infallibility.

In December 1864, two days before the issue of the *Syllabus* (which you remember was on the feast of the Immaculate Conception), the Pope communicated with great secrecy to the Congregation of Rites that the idea of holding a General Council had been long in his mind, as a thing desirable in order to meet the great needs of the Church. During the next two years various cardinals and bishops were consulted. Bishop Dupanloup, at first opposed,[1] came round to approve the project. Satisfied by the results of his tentative approaches, Pius mentioned the design openly in an Allocution on St. Peter's jubilee in June 1867, when bishops were assembled in large numbers in Rome. The precise object of the Council was not revealed. Those who were in the secrets of the Vatican knew that the intention was a definition of Infallibility, and in wider ultramontane circles the hope was cherished that this would be the result of the Council. The bishops who were present at the jubilee in 1867 wished to insert the word *infallible* in their address to the Pontiff, but this was prevented. Archbishop Manning and Senestrey, Bishop of Regensburg, who were at Rome on this occasion, took an oath together to do all in their power, and to offer special prayers every day, for the definition of Papal Infallibility.

Liberal and moderate Catholics like Dupanloup looked forward with great anxiety to the terms of the Papal Bull summoning the Council. It appeared

[1] Pelletier, *Dupanloup*, p. 96; *Collectio Lacensis*, vii. pp. 999 c, ff., 1285 c; Cecconi, Doc. cclxxxi.

a year later, dated June 29, 1868, and it was modelled on the Bull of Paul III. which convoked the Council of Trent. The purpose of the Council was stated to be "most carefully to examine and provide what in these hard times may promote the greater honour of God, the purity of the faith, the dignity of divine service, the salvation of souls, the discipline of secular and regular clergy, their training, the observation of ecclesiastical canons, the improvement of morals, the Christian education of youth, and the common peace and concord of the whole world. So, too, measures shall be most zealously taken to remove all evils from the Church and civil society, to revoke the erring to the right way, to extirpate vice and crime and revive religion."

This vague language might seem to contemplate a discussion of religion and morals in all their aspects. Never before in the annals of the Church had a Council been summoned for such indefinite reasons. Every Council that had ever met had been held to consider some specific question or questions; to settle some disputed point of theology, to condemn some particular heresy, or to deal with some particular abuse. On the face of the Bull, there was no reason for holding a Council then; at any other time the same reasons would have been equally valid. This anomaly, however, was only superficial; it was due to the determination of the Pope and his advisers to preserve official secrecy as to the real object of the Council, which was perfectly definite. The vague language of the Bull was a cloak, and the instructed could read between the lines that the means of compassing all the desirable ends which were enumerated was the definition of Infallibility. Friedrich in his history of the Council has pointed out that the passage of the Bull which I quoted corresponds closely and even verbally to the programme sketched by the Pope in a Brief of 1860 which gave permission to Cardinal Geissel to hold a Provincial Council at Cöln.[1] Cardinal Geissel knew how to interpret it. He drew up a programme of resolutions for that Synod, which closely resembles the scheme adopted afterwards at the Vatican Council, and received (1862) the warm approbation of Pius IX. It included a recognition of the Pope as infallible and as universal bishop. The Bull of Convocation implies these claims elsewhere. Pius subscribes himself as "bishop of the Catholic Church", and he emphasises the absolute jurisdiction of Peter, who is the head, the foundation, and the centre of the Church. Thus to the initiated the Bull said everything; to ordinary clergy and laymen it seemed perfectly innocent. But the very date which was fixed for the opening of the Council was significant and ominous. The 8th of December 1869, the day of the Immaculate Conception, was the date of the issue of the *Syllabus*. These deliberately designed chronological coincidences are an outward symbol of the close inner connexion of the three great acts of the pontificate of Pius IX.

A summons to the Council was issued to the Eastern Church and to the Protestant communities. Rome can hardly have had any illusions that this was a form which could lead to nothing. In his invitation to the Eastern Patriarchs, the Pope avoided

[1] Friedrich, pp. 354 ff.

applying to them the word "schismatics", but the superscription of the letter with the title "the Apostolic Chair" was enough to give offence. It reached the Greek and the Armenian Patriarch at Constantinople, the Coptic Patriarch in Alexandria, the Jacobite Patriarch of Syria and Persia, the Jacobite Bishop of Jerusalem, the Nestorian Patriarch at Kochanes in Kurdistan, and even the Abyssinian Church. Only the Russian Church received no formal invitation. All of them either declined or sent no answer. Among those who did not reply was the Greek Patriarch of Constantinople, but he explained his reasons to the Abbot Testa, who presented the letter, which the Patriarch even refused to receive.[1] He said that he had seen the Bull, which had been printed in the newspapers, and that it contained views which directly contradicted the principles of the Orthodox Church, the spirit of the Gospels, and the doctrines of the Ecumenical Councils. He then went into some of the radical differences between the two Churches, especially the position of the Pope. Finally, he said, if the Western bishops are in doubt and uncertainty on matters of faith, let them hold a council; we have no doubts, we adhere to the unchangeable doctrines derived from the Fathers. And in any case if the Pope of Rome desires a council he should consult the Eastern Patriarchs as equals and brothers, and not signify his will to them as if he were teacher and master of all. The refusal of the Eastern Church to take part deprives the Vatican Council of any real right to the name of Ecumenical.

As to the Protestants. The reply of Prussia was

[1] Friedenberg, pp. 250 f.

to issue circulars for subscriptions and collections to the Gustavus Adolphus Society, which had been founded to support evangelical Churches in Catholic countries.[1] The High Church party in England were unmoved.[2] In 1867 Pusey had said to Bishop Dupanloup "there are 8000 of us in England who pray daily for the unity of the Church", and in the same year 180 clergymen had sought to know from the Pope what would be a possible basis of reunion.[3] The Puseyites had constantly appealed to a General Council, and Rome was at this time keen on recovering England. But to the astonishment of the Jesuits, the Puseyites did not stir when the Council was announced. It could not have been otherwise. Pusey in his "Eirenicon"[4] had designated as the two fundamental grounds of the continuance of the schism, the doctrines of Papal Infallibility and Immaculate Conception; and he now edited a treatise of Turrecremata for the purpose of showing that the proclamation of 1854 was an error which should be corrected at the approaching Council. The attitude of the Puseyites in holding aloof illustrates the words of Dupanloup, who, though he was a believer in Infallibility, thought it a grave mistake to define it. "When the problem is stated", he wrote, "the enemies awaken, the faithful are troubled, the *Protestants draw back*, the governments are disquieted."

[1] Granderath, i. pp. 406-15; *Stimmen aus Maria-Laach*, pp. 164 ff.; *Collectio Lacensis*, vii. p. 1123 d; Cecconi, Doc. cxxiii.; Friedenberg, pp. 253 f.; Frommann, p. 10.

[2] Granderath, i. 397 ff.; Cecconi, i. pp. 262 ff., 293 ff.

[3] Cf. Liddon, *Life of E. B. Pusey*, iv. p. 153.

[4] It was entitled "Is healthful Reunion possible?"

Dr. Cumming, the Scotch Presbyterian, inquired of Archbishop Manning what Protestants must do in order to take part in the Council.[1] Manning inquired at Rome, and the answer was: Return like prodigal children. The Pope afterwards said: Protestantism cannot be discussed, sentence was long ago pronounced, it is a *chose jugée*.[2]

Catholic sovrans had always been invited to General Councils; on this occasion no invitation was sent. Emile Ollivier complained that the Pope by this innovation affirmed the principle of separation between Church and State.[3] The *Univers* said their exclusion proved that they were outside the Church. "In fact, all Catholics are outside the State, which is rotten."[4] At Rome the unsatisfactory explanation was given that the position of Victor Emmanuel, who was excommunicated, caused difficulties; and some princes had violated their Concordats and were consequently ruling over states which had no religion.[5]

The most important event after the publication of the Bull was the appearance on February 6, 1869, of an article in the *Civiltà Catholica*, on the future Council.[6] It was written in France, and expressed

[1] Friedrich, i. pp. 729 ff.; Granderath, i. pp. 399 ff.

[2] *Collectio Lacensis*, pp. 114 f.; Friedenberg, pp. 255 f.

[3] Ollivier, *L'Église et l'État au concile du Vatican*, i. p. 509. Cf. Cecconi, Doc. xxxv. pp. 135 ff.; *Collectio Lacensis*, 7, 1061 b, c.

[4] Veuillot was its editor. Cf. his *Illusion libérale*, pp. 36, 37, 148. On p. 38 we read: "Il n'est point de temps, point de société, point d'homme de qui les fidèles de Jésus-Christ ne doivent exiger, lorsqu'ils le peuvent, quelque forme d'obéissance aux décrets du pontife-roi".

[5] Lagrange, *Dupanloup*, iii. pp. 83 f.; Ollivier, ii. pp. 551 f.

[6] *Collectio Lacensis*, pp. 1147 ff., 1153 ff.; Cecconi, ii. Doc. cxxxv.-cxxxix. Cf. Friedrich, ii. pp. 11-13; Granderath, i. pp. 184-6.

the wish that the Council would confirm the *Syllabus*, carry the definition of Infallibility by acclamation, and declare the dogma of the Virgin's bodily Assumption into heaven. Now the significance of this article as a feeler on the part of the Jesuits has been fully established by the revelation of the official historian of the Council, Cecconi. Towards the end of 1868 the editors of the *Civiltà* approached Antonelli and asked him to direct the Nuncios in the various countries to collect correspondence for their paper on the subject of the Council; and on December 9 Antonelli instructed the Nuncios to this effect, observing that the correspondence thus obtained would both be submitted to the commissions which were preparing the material for the Council and also serve the uses of a journal.[1] Among the points on which communications were invited were the wishes and needs of each country. "Here", wrote Antonelli, "might be indicated points of doctrine or discipline which prelates might like to be decided in the General Council."[2] One of the Nuncios interpreted this to mean whether any new dogmas were desired! Now the article in the *Civiltà* was compiled from correspondence forwarded by Chigi, the Nuncio in Paris.[3] In these circumstances, the quasi-official complexion of the article cannot be called in question. The complaints of the correspondents as to the use made of their letters were hushed up; and when some of the ambassadors spoke

[1] *Collectio Lacensis*, pp. 1048 b, ff., 1061 b, c; Cecconi, Doc. xxxv. pp. 135 ff.

[2] *Collectio Lacensis*, pp. 1146 c, ff.; Cecconi, ii. Doc. cxxxv.

[3] Friedrich, ii. pp. 10 ff.

to the Pope or Antonelli on the subject, they denied all responsibility for the *Civiltà*.

The article which disclosed the true objects of the Council to the world called forth the famous articles of Döllinger[1] in the Augsburger *Allgemeine Zeitung*, entitled "The Council and the *Civiltà*", which were published in March 1869. The most learned ecclesiastical historian in Germany, he pointed out what the definition of Papal Infallibility would mean, what changes it would introduce in the Church, how it would raise the propositions of the *Syllabus* to authoritative dogma; and he tried to show that it would affect the whole modern world. He prophesied what the character and procedure of the Council would be, and it is remarkable how his predictions were verified. "In 449", he said, "a synod was held which got the name of the synod of robbers; the Council of 1869 will be the synod of flatterers."[2] "If the Council allows itself to be used to bind the

[1] On his attitude cf. his *Kleinere Schriften* (ed. Reusch), pp. 357 ff.; Michael, *Döllinger*, p. 55. His theory is specially plain in the *Allgemeine Zeitung*, March 11, 1870. Cf. *Collectio Lacensis*, vii. p. 1502 a; Schulte, *Die Stellung der Konzilien*, p. 104; Lagrange, *Dupanloup*, iii. pp. 131 ff.; Friedrich, *Döllinger*, iii. p. 498.

[2] *Allgemeine Zeitung* (Augsburg), 1869, No. 74, 1126. Döllinger's sixty-nine letters were published at Munich in 1870 just as they appeared in the *Allgemeine Zeitung*. Friedrich edited them. There is an authorised English version entitled *Quirinus, Letters from Rome on the Council*. The date of the first letter is December 1869, and of the sixty-ninth July 19, 1870. Cf. Friedrich, *Döllinger*, iii. pp. 518 ff.; Michael, *Döllinger*, p. 107. The three friends of these letters are Friedrich, Döllinger, and Acton. Manning, with reason, regarded Acton almost as dangerous as Döllinger. According to Friedrich, Strossmayer was one of the main inspirers of these famous letters (Friedrich, *Döllinger*, iii. pp. 549, 703). Figgis and Laurence edited vol. i. of *Lord Acton's Correspondence*, and it is invaluable for the understanding of Ultramontanism. Its publishers tell me that there will not be a second volume.

wreath of Infallibility round the Pope's brow, none of those consequences will ensue which followed the fifth Lateran Council (which preceded the Reformation). There will be no great and sudden rebellion, no insurrection in the grand style; all will remain quiet, only too quiet. The Jesuits and their pupils will sing Hosanna, draw some inferences from the dogma and use it for their purposes; and the world will look on indifferent. But a deep antipathy against the Italian priesthood will gradually grow."[1]

The article in the *Civiltà* also led to action on the part of the Bavarian minister, Prince Hohenlohe, who was intimate with Döllinger. He sent a circular on April 9, 1869, to the Bavarian envoys, instructing them to call the attention of the governments to the Council and propose united action, so that the Pope might know in time what the attitude of the Powers would be.[2] But the proposal met with no sympathy.[3] The attitude of the governments was that if the Council should make any encroachments, it would be time enough to think of acting. Arnim—Prussian ambassador at Munich—ridiculed Hohenlohe, said he was inspired by Döllinger, and that the

[1] *Allegmeine Zeitung* (Augsburg), No. 74, 1126. Cf. Friedrich, ii. pp. 21 ff.

[2] *Collectio Lacensis*, pp. 1199 ff.; Cecconi, ii. Doc. clxix.; Friedenberg, pp. 354 f. Prince Hohenlohe, in his *Memoirs*, reveals that Döllinger drafted the body of this circular. Had Prince Hohenlohe's advice been taken, the Vatican might not improbably have hesitated to challenge a conflict with Roman Catholic Europe. But it did not at that moment suit Bismarck to follow this advice; Beust was far too superficial to comprehend its drift; France was distracted by internal troubles; and the peculiar conditions of Italy rendered it impossible for her to interfere.

[3] Friedrich, *Döllinger*, iii. pp. 487 ff.; Cecconi, Doc. clxxiii.

question was merely theological.[1] The President of the Swiss Federal Council also asked Prussia what it intended to do.[2] Bismarck said he did not share in the hopes or anxieties of others; the Council would not touch the political interests of Prussia.[3]

The anonymous articles in the *Allgemeine Zeitung* were enlarged and recast in book form by Döllinger and Huber, and appeared in July under the pseudonym of *Janus*. The book was a systematic historical criticism of Papal Infallibility; it traced the gradual growth of ultramontane doctrines, and dealt with the fabrications on which they had been based. Archbishop Ketteler of Mainz, who was personally opposed to the definition of Infallibility, said that Janus had only one parallel for untruth—the *Provincial Letters* of Pascal.[4] Bishop Hergenrother of Wurzburg wrote a reply entitled *Anti-Janus*—an extremely weak performance.

In Germany, outside the theological school of Munich, there were not a great number who rejected the doctrine of Infallibility itself, but there were a great many who, like Archbishop Ketteler, were strongly convinced that its definition was inopportune. This opinion was expressed by the majority of an assembly of bishops who met at Fulda.[5] The same position was held by a considerable number of the French bishops, including Dupanloup,[6] who

[1] *Collectio Lacensis*, p. 1203 c; Cecconi, Doc. clxxix.; Ollivier, i. p. 513.

[2] *Collectio Lacensis*, pp. 1215 b, ff.; Cecconi, Doc. clxxxvii.

[3] *Collectio Lacensis*, pp. 1202 d, ff., 1209 c, ff.

[4] Friedrich, i. pp. 367, 626-8. Ketteler's letter is in *Collectio Lacensis*, p. 1485.

[5] Granderath, i. pp. 232-46; Friedrich, ii. pp. 200 ff.; *Collectio Lacensis*, 7, pp. 1196 a, ff.

[6] Falloux, ii. pp. 418 ff.

worked hard to avert the danger and drew down upon himself all the venom of the editor of the *Univers*.

No one worked harder or took a more prominent part in bringing about the accomplishment of the Pope's wishes than Archbishop Manning.[1] He had very slight theological or historical equipment, but he made up for these defects by boldness and enthusiasm. In October 1869 he published a pastoral letter which assumed the proportions of a book, entitled *The Oecumenical Council and the Infallibility of the Roman Pontiff*. The well-known intimacy of the author with the Vatican lent the publication great importance; but it was only after the Council that Manning acknowledged that one chapter was not his own, but was furnished by the official committee which was preparing the material for the Council. This shows how deeply, though not a member of the committee, Manning was initiated into the secrets. The purpose of the work is to prove that the definition of Infallibility is opportune. He answers objections and advances positive arguments. One notes such curious sophisms as this. The Church is the body, and the Pope is the head; the Church is infallible, but an infallible body with a fallible head is absurd; therefore the head is infallible. Of course, the correct Catholic doctrine in regard to the Early Councils was that the body and head together, but

[1] The main source for his activities is Purcell, *Life of Cardinal Manning*, vol. ii., chapters xvi. and xvii. Purcell should be read in the more candid first edition. Cecconi, Friedrich, and Granderath naturally devote much space to the man termed by the Italian papers "Il Diavolo del Concilio". One of the best etched sketches of Manning is by Ollivier, *L'Église et l'État*, ii. pp. 8 ff. Lytton Strachey has subtly portrayed him in his *Eminent Victorians*.

neither separately, were infallible. Manning says that an urgent reason for not leaving the Infallibility question longer in *suspense* is that in the history of the Church many decisions were made by Popes, which were not decreed by Councils, and it ought to be determined whether there is any doubt about their validity. For instance, he says, the decision of Innocent I. as to original sin and the doctrine of Pope Gelasius as to the Canon of Holy Scriptures. Here Manning shows his imperfect acquaintance with the history of theology. Gelasius laid down no doctrine about the Canon; in the decree which goes by his name there is merely an enumeration of scriptural books. And when Manning wrote, it had already been recognised by critics, like Hefele, that this part of the decree was older; it was the work of Pope Damasus. And then when we go back to Pope Damasus things do not look very favourable to the cause of Infallibility, for the canon of Damasus ascribed to St. John the Evangelist only one letter, the other two being attributed to another person of the same name; whereas Pope Innocent ascribed all three letters to the Apostle. Here are two Infallibles in contradiction with one another. But the accuracy about facts really did not matter for Manning's position or purpose. It is high time, he says, that the pretensions of historical science should be confined to its own sphere. That will be done by the Council with the help of the Holy Ghost! During the Council, he put this briefly: "The dogma must conquer history".[1]

[1] Cf. his *Temporal Mission of the Holy Ghost*, pp. 28, 203, 226, especially p. 226. There he says that "the appeal to antiquity is

Now while the Church was agitated with excitement and anxieties and the Papal Court was occupied with preparations for the Council, Italy was waiting for the first opportunity to seize Rome. If the opportunity came and Victor Emmanuel moved before December 1869, the Council could not be held. It was the presence of French troops in the Roman State that stood in the way, and the great object of the diplomacy of Florence was to have them removed. The question became the subject of secret negotiations between France, Austria, and Italy in 1868. It was not the prospect of the Council that influenced these governments, but the result of their negotiations was to decide whether the Council could be held. Rouher's famous asseveration in the Chamber that "Italy would never go to Rome" had marked the collapse, at the end of 1867, of previous *pourparlers* between the same three powers, through the attitude of France.[1] But Napoleon, foreseeing a conflict with Prussia, was holding out his hand to Italy in 1868, and Austria, when she learned of the possibility of an alliance, determined to be a third.[2] The Austrian war party, of which the Archduke Albrecht was the leader, was thirsting for revenge on Prussia.[3] The negotiations were first of all en-

---

both a treason and a heresy. It is a treason, because it rejects the Divine voice of the Church *at this hour*; and a heresy, because it denies that voice to be divine." Cf. Manning's letter to *The Daily Telegraph*, October 8, 1875.

[1] *Allgemeine Zeitung* (Augsburg), December 9, 1867.

[2] Prince Jerome Napoleon, "Les alliances de l'empire en 1869 et 1870", *Revue des deux Mondes*, 1878, xxvi. pp. 489-500; *Journal des Débats*, May 14, 1878; Mérimée, *Lettres*, ii. pp. 354-5.

[3] Friedrich, III. ii. p. 676.

tirely conducted by the sovrans themselves. When they had reached a general agreement on the conditions of a triple alliance, then ministers had to be taken into their confidence and the matter passed into their hands. But as soon as this had happened, the Roman question, on which the sovrans had only touched very delicately, became crucial. Italy demanded, in return for her effective help, that the Roman question should be settled, through the withdrawal of the French troops. In this demand Count Beust, the Austrian Chancellor, strongly supported Italy; he showed himself a determined enemy of the temporal power.[1] It was a novel position for Austria to assume. But when the Italian government required France to return to the September Convention, the French minister, De Lavalette, informed it that Napoleon did not feel able to execute that convention, that the negotiation must be suspended, but might be resumed at a more favourable opportunity. This was in June 1869. The sovrans indeed continued to interchange letters.

These diplomatic transactions were virtually a secret from the world, and it is impossible to say how much the Vatican knew about them; but there was certainly considerable apprehension at Rome as to the eventuality of the French troops being withdrawn. The action of Napoleon in breaking off the negotiation was decisive; to him belongs the credit of having made the Vatican Council possible. Personally, of course, he did not want the Council. His action was only another proof of his weakness, and

[1] Ollivier, *L'Église et l'État*, ii. pp. 473-4; D'Ideville, *Les Piemontais à Rome*, chap. viii.

the weakness of his political position; he was depending more and more on the clerical party. In October the Italian minister, Menabrea, sent round a circular in which he observed: The Italian government cannot avoid considering it a fact of great importance that France is assuring her protection to an assembly directed against Italy by permitting French troops to form the garrison of the Church State during the session of the Council. In January 1870 Bismarck observed: "France has the Council entirely in her hands, and she can endanger it by withdrawing her troops".[1] Frenchmen have not been unconscious of the responsibility incurred by their country in facilitating the enactment of decrees which caused much unrest in European states; but the attempts of Émile Ollivier, the apologist of the Second Empire, to justify French policy are curiously unconvincing.[2]

The French government indeed went somewhat further. In the instruction sent to De la Tour d'Auvergne, the envoy at Rome, it went so far as to countenance a definition of Infallibility.[3] The document runs: "For some years past there is a movement in the Catholic Church, aiming at augmenting unduly the prerogatives of the Pope and even proclaiming as dogma his personal Infallibility". This sounds promising; but how does it go

[1] Despatch of January 5, 1870, in Friedenberg, p. 524; Ollivier, i. 388 ff., 398, 519-28, 530, ii. pp. 29 ff.; Rothan, *L'Allemagne et l'Italie*, ii. p. 84; Cadorna, *La Liberazione di Roma*, p. 361.

[2] Cf. *Collectio Lacensis*, pp. 1216 b, 1218 a, 1220 c, 1229 a; Cecconi, Doc. clxxxviii.

[3] Ollivier, i. p. 519; *Collectio Lacensis*, pp. 1233 d, 1234 c; Maynard, pp. 192 f.; Ollivier, i. pp. 519 f.; ii. p. 29.

on? "There is no doubt that the doctrine of the Infallibility of the Pope speaking *ex cathedra* admits many subtle distinctions, and we have reason to hope that if an explanation on this matter must be given, the expression will be chosen with extreme discretion."[1] Thus the government of Napoleon did what no other government did; it countenanced a discreet definition of Infallibility. Ollivier calls the French policy a policy of abstention;[2] it was really a policy of surrender to the ultramontane party.[3]

While Rome preserved official silence as to the precise object of the Council and what it was to do, many bishops and theologians published pamphlets, offering their opinions on what subjects should be discussed and proposing programmes. I may mention the work of Professor Walter of Bonn on *The General Council and the Ecumenical Situation*,[4] which deprecated the consideration of Papal prerogatives or of anti-Christian errors as futile, and called attention to questions of jurisdiction and discipline, and especially the establishment of a *modus vivendi* with the modern state. Ratzinger's book on *The next General Council and the true needs of the Church*, published anonymously, sketched a more ambitious programme, but one which was even more offensive to the ultramontanes and the *Civiltà Catholica*.[5] One of the great objects, he said, ought to be to reinstate all the Christian Confessions; the invitation of the non-Catholics was good, but they

[1] *Collectio Lacensis*, 1234 c.
[2] I. p. 391. This page is decisive.
[3] I. pp. 530, 531. Cf. Granderath's comments, II. ii. pp. 369 ff.
[4] *Das allgemeine Concilium u. die Weltlage* (Regensburg, 1869).
[5] Friedrich, ii. pp. 20, 285-93.

should not only be invited but listened to; and the basis of reunion should be the Apostles' Creed and the doctrines on which all Christians are unanimous. Another object should be to make provision that the clergy should receive an education which would place them abreast of the most advanced culture and science of the age. Their training should not be confined to scholasticism, liturgy, and ritual; they must study history impartially, and the *Index Librorum* prohibitions must be abolished. Another question of pressing importance was the reformation of Church government in both head and members. This section of the book is extremely drastic. All nations of the Christian world should exercise equal influence on the election of the Pope; there is no good reason or right why the Pontificate should be confined to Italians. The Congregations must also be reformed; the Congregation of the Inquisition must be done away with as well as that of the Index. Further, the Pope must banish from his Court the avariciousness which has become proverbial. This book was at first ascribed to Döllinger. It was generally thought even by the most liberal Catholics that while there was much truth in it, it was too rough and unsparing.

Of other works I need only refer to that of Professor Ginzel of Leitmeritz, entitled *Reform of the Roman Church in its Head and in its Members*, a very ominous title, which called down the wrath of Vatican circles.[1] It is enough to say that it was a free and radical criticism, and that it strongly denounced the dominant theory of the relations of

[1] Friedrich, ii. pp. 207-8, 296-303. Ginzel enjoyed the confidence of Cardinal Schwarzenberg.

Church to State, which maintained still the principle of the *Unam Sanctam* of Boniface VIII.[1]

It is observed that the ultramontanes of Germany, Austria, and Switzerland did not publish any proposals or programmes for the Council. It was part of their position that the initiative should lie with the Pope.

Hardly anything in the nature of proposals appeared in France, where theological learning was at low ebb; Italy was almost equally unproductive. An Englishman, Urquhart, who was an Anglican and editor of the *Diplomatic Review*, published some articles in the spring of 1868, which attracted considerable attention.[2] They were entitled "How the Ecumenical Council may act on the human race"; "The Ecumenical Council: Restoration of the Law of Nations"; "Appeal of a Protestant to the Pope to restore the Law of Nations". His idea was that the cause of the chief evils of the age was due to the decline of law, and the remedy was to restore respect for the Law of Nations. This, he held, could only be done by the Pope or the Council. Law, he said, is based on the Ten Commandments, and it is everyone's duty to maintain it, but especially the Pope's. It is his duty as king to protest against all acts of violence. If his government undertakes the protection of justice, it will become the most powerful on earth.[3]

This will suffice to show what his idea was. As it tended to exalt the power and importance of Popes,

[1] Published in 1302.

[2] Granderath, i. p. 400; *Collectio Lacensis*, vii. pp. 1309 c, ff.

[3] Friedrich, ii. pp. 329-33.

and emanated from a non-Catholic, it was received with respect and attention by the Vatican, and by the Catholic press of all countries. It was indeed a return to the mediaeval idea of the Pope. The Jesuit organs praised it, but, of course, their idea was to restore his mediaeval position through the halo of Infallibility.[1]

The literature on the Vatican Council is very extensive. To some of the most remarkable examples of the pamphlet literature which circulated before its assembly, I have referred. On the histories of the Council itself some like that of Pressensé may be neglected. That of Cardinal Manning threw light on some points, but it must be used with great precaution. The three most important histories are the quasi-official *Storia del Concilio* by Archbishop Cecconi; the history of Plantier, which was approved of by the Pope; and the *History of the Vatican Council* by Friedrich, which is far the best. It is bitterly anti-Papal, but it gives the facts accurately, and the author had an unrivalled survey of all the literature bearing on his subject. He was a trained ecclesiastical historian, a pupil of Döllinger, and made a special study of Conciliar history, especially of the Council of Trent. He was invited to act as theological adviser of Cardinal Hohenlohe, the brother of the Bavarian minister, at the Council, and he was at Rome in that capacity all the time.[2] He kept a careful diary of his experiences, which lets us see the various phases of opinion, the fears

[1] *Stimmen aus Maria-Laach*, i. 4, pp. 130 f., 135; Cecconi, ii. pp. 333 ff.

[2] Friedrich, *Tagebuch während des vatikan. Konzils*, p. 1.

and the anxieties of the minority, their vacillations and compromises. The ultramontanes would have been glad to find an excuse for driving him from Rome. He was looked on askance for his learning and for his connexion with Döllinger and the Munich school of theology; and his employment by Cardinal Hohenlohe, whose brother was so strongly opposed to the Council, did not recommend him. Besides Friedrich, Bishop Hefele was almost the only man at Rome who had a profound knowledge of ecclesiastical history. The majority of the Fathers were grossly ignorant, or possessed a superficial knowledge derived from handbooks. It was the aim of the Vatican to discourage them from studying history during the Council. We shall see that the Vatican librarian Thenier had special orders not to permit anyone to examine the *Acta Concilii Tridentini*.[1]

[1] Friedrich, III. ii. pp. 1039, 1096.

IV

THE VATICAN COUNCIL

THE work of the Council was being carefully prepared at Rome for over two years.[1] It was important to obtain the co-operation of theologians who had fame for learning. The name of Newman naturally occurred; but Manning and the Jesuits succeeded in excluding him.[2] The work was organised in the form of a *Directing Congregation* and six committees. Cardinal Patrizi was president of the Congregation, which included Sanguinetti the Jesuit, Monsignor Talbot, and the learned Hefele, Bishop of Rottenburg. Of the committees the most important was the Dogmatic. Its president was Luigi Bilio (who,

[1] The two principal official collections of documents are Eugenio Cecconi, *Storia del concilio ecumenico vaticano scritta sui documenti originali,* Rome, 1873–9, 4 vols., and Gerhard Schneeman and Théodore Granderath, *Acta et decreta Sacrosancti Oecumenici Concili Vaticani. Accedunt permulta alia documenta ad Concilium ejusque historiam spectantia,* Freiburg, 1892, vol. 7. The latter I generally cite as *Collectio Lacensis* and a few times as *Acta.* In 1872, E. Friedenberg published his useful *Sammlung der Aktenstücke zum ersten vatikanischen Konzil mit einem Grundrisse der Geschichte desselben.* Bishop Martin published his *Collectio omnium documentorum concilii Vaticani* in 1873. J. Friedrich's *Documenta ad illustrandum Concilium Vaticanum anni 1870* is also useful. Cf. Mirbt's admirable article in the *Historische Zeitschrift,* vol. v., series iii. (1908), on the "Geschichtsschreibung des vatikan. Konzil".

[2] *Sull' opportunità della definizione dommatica dell' Infall.* (Napoli, 1869), p. 9; Icard, *Journal,* pp. 278-9.

you remember, had been concerned in the compilation of the *Syllabus* and who had been made a Cardinal); it included the Jesuits Perrone and Schrader, whose names are also associated with the *Syllabus*. The members were sworn to secrecy. Each member of this committee had to draw up a report on a given subject—some point of doctrine which had led to heresy. Heresies were to be traced, formulated, and reasons given for their condemnation. From all these reports the committee compiled a *Schema de fide* which was to be laid before the Council.

The Council was to be opened on December 8. But it had been decided that a preliminary Assembly should be held on December 2 as a sort of a preface, and on that day the Bishops and members of the Council who had already arrived in Rome gathered in the Sistine Chapel; they numbered 503, including 43 Cardinals. The Pope delivered an address in which he virtually identified his own voice with that of Christ; but it was disappointing to the audience, who hoped to hear definitely what the programme of the Council would be. It consisted entirely of phrases. After the address, a Papal Brief was read fixing the order of proceedings and the mode in which the Council was to be conducted.[1]

(I must note here that on the same day, December 2, official notices were posted on the doors of St. Peter, Sta. Maria Sopra Minerva, the Inquisition Palace, and the Curia Innocentiana, that the book entitled *Janus* had been condemned by the Index Congregation, and that their decision was confirmed by the Pope.)

[1] *Collectio Lacensis*, 17 ff.; Friedenberg, pp. 358 ff.

To return to the order of proceedings. It was a complete and high-handed innovation that this should be prescribed by the Pope, and not fixed by the Council itself.[1] It was ordained that there were to be three kinds of meetings: (1) committees which were to prepare the decrees, (2) general congregations which were to pass the decrees, and (3) public sessions which were to publish them.

In his Brief the Pope claimed the exclusive right of initiating proposals, a right which had not been claimed at Trent or any former Council.[2] He announced, however, that he would allow the Fathers to share in this privilege. But the concession was rendered futile by the provision that if a member wished to make a proposal he must submit it first to a committee appointed by the Pope, and the Pope would decide whether the proposal should be discussed. Under such novel limitations it could not be said that the Council was a free body in the sense in which this could be said of other Councils. The restriction on the right of proposing was a violation of what may be called Conciliar law, as shown by the practice at the Ecumenical Councils and at the Council of Trent. At the latter Council an attempt had been made to appropriate to the Pope or his

[1] Friedrich, *Tagebuch*, pp. 11 ff., yet cf. Fessler, p. 34. Cf. also *Aktenst.* ii. pp. 29 ff.; Acton, pp. 50 ff.; Friedenberg, p. 97; Fessler, *Das vatic. Concil*, pp. 31 ff.

[2] Friedrich, iii. p. 86; Fessler, p. 51; *Collectio Lacensis*, pp. 1551 b, 917 ff. Cf. the last, pp. 489, 778, 1077, 1087; Ollivier, i. p. 500; Lagrange, *Dupanloup*, iii. p. 55. Cf. Figgis and Laurence, *Lord Acton's Correspondence*, i. pp. 89-90: "The sole legislative authority has been abandoned to the Pope. It includes the right of issuing dogmatic decrees, and involves the possession of all the infallibility which the Church claims."

legates the right of proposing, but it had been successfully resisted.

Another innovation of great importance which was introduced was the requirement of strict secrecy as to the proceedings of the Council. The words of the Brief are as follows: "Considerations of policy cause us to ordain that throughout the whole duration of the Council official secrecy shall be observed; in view of the seriousness of present circumstances this must be prescribed more than in the case of former Councils. This foresight is highly necessary at the present time when godlessness, equipped with a thousand weapons of destruction, is on the watch to lose no opportunity of stirring up odium against the Catholic Church and its doctrines. Therefore, we command all the fathers, the officials of the Council, the theologians, the canonists, and all who perform any official services at the Council not to reveal to any outside person decrees or any business discussed, or the opinions of individual members. Officials, who are not members, must take an oath of secrecy."[1]

This instruction came as a great surprise.[2] It placed the members in a very awkward position. They came to Rome without any information as to the subjects which were to be discussed, so that they had not been able to study the questions beforehand.

[1] Par. 3 of "Multiplices inter", laying down the ordering of business at the Vatican Council. Cf. Quirinus, *Letters . . . on the Council*, p. 13.

[2] Fessler, p. 35. Cf. Bishop Strossmayer's striking testimony to the absence of freedom at the Council in his letter of November 27, 1870. It was first printed in the *Deutsche Merkur*, and was reprinted in the *Kölnische Zeitung*, July 13, 1881.

Every member was now debarred from consulting anyone except the theologian whom he had brought with him. If there was a man of learning in his own diocese whose opinion he would have valued on a theological point, he could not communicate with him. And special precautions were taken to prevent this. The Papal post office was empowered to stop letters, and send them to the censor. It was also explained by the Secretary of the Council, Bishop Fessler, that the theologians were precluded from attending private meetings of bishops, and afterwards even meetings of bishops were subjected to restrictions. The members of the Council were forbidden to print anything on the subject of the Council either at Rome or elsewhere. Thus the Pope and his advisers were determined to shroud the proceedings of the Council in deep obscurity, until its final result should be published to the world. The intention was that the *acta* should never be known except in an official history.

There was yet another significant innovation announced in the Brief. All the decrees were to be introduced by the words: "Pius, bishop, servant of God, with the approbation of the Sacred Council, ordains".[1] The decrees were thus to be in the name of the Pope. At Trent the formula was: "The sacred Synod, lawfully assembled in the Holy Ghost, under the presidency of the legates of the Apostolic See, ordains".[2] By accepting this form the Council

[1] *Collectio Lacensis*, p. 56; "Multiplices inter", § 8. Cf. Schulte, *Stellung*, pp. 81 ff.

[2] *Acta Congregationum*, i. p. 39. Cf. Friedrich, iii. pp. 70 ff., and contrast Fessler, *Das vatikanische Konzilium*, p. 39; Hinschius, *Kirchenrecht*, iii. p. 362; Cecconi, i. pp. 244, 246.

implicitly admitted that the Pope was independent of the Council, that the Council was superfluous and was not a Council in any real sense.

The meeting place arranged for the Council was in the right transept of St. Peter's Church. The Pope was insistent that the sessions should be held close to the Apostle's tomb. It was fitted up like an aula. But for practical purposes a worse place for a large assembly to deliberate could not have been selected. The acoustic properties were extremely bad, and a discussion which should be audible to all was impossible. Many complaints were made, and there was talk of providing better accommodation in the Quirinal, but nothing was done. Before the Council opened, there had been a trial of the acoustic properties of the aula, at which the Pope was present. The Bishop of Aire ascended the pulpit and sonorously declaimed a definition of Infallibility which amused the Pope.[1] He was no doubt satisfied that the aula was adequate for promulgating the definition, and nothing more was necessary.

The Cardinal von Reisach was appointed President of the Council, but he died soon after it opened, and the Cardinal de Angelis succeeded him.[2] It is unnecessary to describe the long and ceremonious opening session on December 8, at which the Pope was present, delivered an address, and recommended the Council to the mother of God. 719 members had assembled, and in January this number swelled by late arrivals to 744. Of the European members, who

[1] *The Vatican*, p. 23.

[2] Acton, *Zur Geschichte des vatikanischen Konzils*, p. 67; Schulte, *Stellung der Konzilien*, p. 254.

counted 541, more than half were Italians. There were 113 Americans, 13 Australians, 14 Africans, and 83 Asiatics.

In the days following the preliminary meeting, the general surprise and dismay occasioned by the ordinances which the Papal Brief laid down for the Council threw everything else into the background. The chagrin was felt not only by the men who were opposed to the extreme Roman claims, but by the general rank and file of French and German bishops who were ready to vote for anything the Pope wished. But they were conscious of the indignity of sharing in a Council from which even the semblance of freedom was taken away. The nomination of the secretary and all the officers of the Council by the Pope, as well as his exclusive privilege of initiation, produced a painful impression.

But the question of Infallibility, though as yet there was no official knowledge that it would be brought forward, operated during these first days in grouping the members. Before the opening meeting of December 8, the fathers were instinctively differentiating themselves into two large sections —a majority which was in favour of the definition of Infallibility, and a minority opposed to it. And within the majority national groups were formed. For instance, the Spanish bishops met almost immediately under the chairmanship of Cardinal Moreno, and resolved to vote for everything that was submitted to the Council, especially Infallibility, and, if Infallibility were not brought forward by others, to endeavour to secure its definition.

It is not necessary to describe the great opening

meeting on December 8, at which the Pope was present and delivered an address, but it was not entirely satisfactory to the Pope. He had appointed the Archbishop of Iconium, Pücher-Passavalli, to preach the sermon on this occasion, and sent him a private hint that he should emphasise the desirability of sanctioning Infallibility as an article of faith at the Council. But although the Cardinal's hat had been promised him, Passavalli ignored the intimation, and did not say a word on the subject in his sermon.[1]

The first Congregation met on December 10, and an announcement was made of the names of the Commission who were appointed to examine any motions which members of the Council wished to bring forward.[2] The names were almost entirely those of known Infallibilists: they included Moreno, leader of the Spanish party, Riario Sforza of the Italian, Bonnechose of the French, Cullen of the Irish; also Manning and Dechamps (of Malines), the most eminent literary advocates of the doctrine; and Bishop Martin of Paderborn, a red-hot Infallibilist.[3] Of the twenty-six there were only three opponents, one of whom was Cardinal Rauscher, Archbishop of Vienna, but their views were unknown at the time. A Bull was then read to the Assembly, which provided that, if the Pope died during the Council, the Council should be suspended and have no voice in the election, which should rest as usual with the

[1] *Collectio Lacensis*, 764 d, ff.; Friedrich, ii. p. 425; III. i. p. 129. The sermon is in Friedenberg, pp. 366 ff.

[2] Cf. Friedrich, iii. pp. 166-9, 175 ff., 177.

[3] Granderath gives the different lists, ii. pp. 96-9. Cf. Friedrich, III. i. pp. 236 ff.

Cardinals, and the Council should not meet again till summoned by the new Pope. This created considerable dissatisfaction. The fathers were annoyed at the acoustic deficiencies of the hall. Some said in voting *non placet quia nihil intelleximus*, but most, out of respect to Pius, pretended to hear.[1]

The Bull for the next papal election had perhaps the effect of consolidating the minority, and some incidents which happened outside the Council contributed to this. For instance, Cardinal Schwarzenberg, one of the most prominent anti-Infallibilists, had an audience of the Pope and brought forward some of his objections to Infallibility. The Pope replied: "I, Giovanni Maria Mastai, believe in Infallibility. As Pope I have nothing to ask from the Council; the Holy Ghost will enlighten it."[2] It soon became clear that the minority was about 120 strong, and, including the Oriental bishops, amounted to 150. The size of the minority would at least render it impossible to carry decrees by acclamation.

According to the instructions of the Papal Brief, four commissions were to be chosen by the Council for preparing the business in four different departments. The first was to deal with dogma, the second with ecclesiastical discipline, the third with the affairs of religious orders, the fourth with the Oriental Churches. The first, under which Infallibility came, was the most important. It was of the greatest

[1] Granderath, ii. p. 68; Darboy, *La Liberté*, p. 139; Pomponio Leto, p. 64.

[2] Cf. Ollivier, ii. p. 336. This utterance is in Friedrich, III. i. pp. 108 f. Take another utterance: "As to Infallibility, I believed it as plain Abbé Mastai, and now, as Pope Mastai, I FEEL it" (Quirinus, p. 132). Cf. Friedenberg, *Aktenstücke*, p. 108; Friedrich, III. i. p. 649.

consequence for the future of the Council how these commissions should be composed, especially the first; and the crucial point was whether members of the minority should be admitted.

On this question the editor of the *Univers* wrote on December 14: "The Majority and Minority at a Council are not analogous to political coalitions, in which the exclusion of members of our party is justifiable. If this were done it would seem like an attempt to make the Holy Ghost lie, and would be branded as a repulsive intrigue." But this was not the view of the Pope and the Curia. We are enlightened on this by Plantier, the historian approved by the Pope. His words are quite candid: "Among the bishops of the minority", he says, "there were men of prominence who had deserved well of the Holy See and the Church, men distinguished for learning and eloquence. They had a right to be included in the Commissions, and would have enriched them with stores of learning. But their writings and speeches, in fact everything, show that in the great question of Infallibility they held stubbornly to views which were obsolete and had been a hundred times condemned. They had announced that they would oppose any decree which contradicted those views. That was enough. They were inexorably excluded from committees which were open to men of less reputation, but who represented a purer faith and sounder theology. Certain elements, in short, were mercilessly excluded."[1] He then goes on to designate the majority and the committees they elected as a great army well ordered

[1] C. H. Plantier in Roskovány, *Monumenta Catholica*, vii. pp. 649 f. Cf. his *Les Conciles généraux et le concile du Vatican*.

for battle. There is no doubt that the elections were made by means of lists prepared beforehand, though the episcopate of any country in which Infallibilists were more numerous had a free hand to select the names they wished. It is to be noted that Manning used all his influence to exclude the non-Infallibilists; they are heretics, he said, in the position of a cursed person, and must only be permitted to discuss and defend themselves. The voting for the dogmatic Committee was held on the 14th and the result published on the 17th. The list contained hardly any well-known names; the various nations were impartially represented; but as Manning's paper, *The Vatican*, observed: "Not one member was compromised by Gallican or liberal principles. Of the twenty-four every one is distinguished by devotion to the Chair of St. Peter, or, to speak in the modern phrase, by ultramontane doctrines and sympathies."[1] The less important Committee for ecclesiastical discipline, of which the names were published on the 23rd, contained only two, and those not prominent, members of the minority. The results in the case of the other committees, which were elected later, were similar.

There is no doubt that the majority were surprised at the number of the minority. Manning and others found it genuinely difficult to understand their attitude, or to conceive how so many Catholic bishops could combine to oppose the wishes of the Pope and cause him anxiety and annoyance. But if Pius was vexed at the resistance and the obstacles which were presented to his hopes of a speedy and triumphant promulgation of the dogma, at the same

[1] Cf. Friedrich, III. i. pp. 165-7.

time the fact that a minority was formed, comprising very influential prelates, corroborated his belief in the prophecies of Anna Maria Taigi. For that inspired sibyl, in foretelling that Papal Infallibility would be defined at a Council under the auspices of Pius IX., had also declared that it would be opposed by some of the most eminent ecclesiastics in the Church.[1] Meanwhile he was amiable to members of the opposition. He gave (December 22) a long audience to Ketteler of Mainz,[2] one of the most prominent of the Inopportunists. He opened the interview with the words *Amas me?* Ketteler, like St. Peter, was confused, but answered with expressions of devotion. But he explained his views on the question of opportunism, and left the sacred presence unconverted.[3]

The minority meanwhile were taking counsel together, though not in a very business-like or effective way. It was determined to present an address to the Pope demanding free initiation in making proposals:[4] Strossmayer drew it up,[5] but some of the most important bishops, who had approved of the design at first, refused to sign it for various reasons. It never led to anything.[6]

From December 17 letters began to appear in the Augsburg *Allgemeine Zeitung* (a journal which stank in the nostrils of the Vatican) on the "First Days of the Council". They excited the indignation not only of the majority but also of the minority, but they

[1] Callisto, *Vita della V.S. di Dio A. M. Taigi*, pp. 206 ff.

[2] His *Freiheit, Autoritat u. Kirche* is well worth reading.

[3] Quirinus, *Letters . . . on the Council*, p. 139.

[4] Friedrich, III. i. p. 231.

[5] Friedrich, *Documenta*, ii. pp. 380 f.

[6] *Ibid.* i. p. 136.

were greedily read at Rome, and Antonelli had to get them translated into Italian. It had been hoped that no news about the proceedings had escaped beyond the members and the initiated at Rome, but these articles withdrew the veil of secrecy. All the actors were displayed on the stage, and the secrets of the Vatican and the mandates of the two parties were disclosed. The articles showed a knowledge far wider and more intimate of what was going on than most of the members of the Council possessed. The tone was critical and often sarcastic; individuals were not spared; the weak points of the authorities were exposed. From December 27 they appeared under the name *Roman Letters on the Council,* and everyone at Rome who wished to know the secret threads which were being twined, and the intrigues which were being woven, around him, had to read them. The question was: Who wrote them? Suspicion alighted for a moment on the attaché of the Bavarian Embassy, Count Louis von Arco, and also on Lord Acton.[1] But they finally concentrated themselves on the Palazzo Valentini, the residence of Cardinal Hohenlohe, and ascribed the authorship to Professor Friedrich. Hohenlohe's residence was regarded as the focus of opposition, and the belief in Friedrich's responsibility for the letters intensified the distrust of the Bavarian Cardinal's house. Friedrich absolutely denied the charge; he says that the letters could not have been the work of one person alone.

The appearance of these letters demanded, on the part of the Vatican, counter operations in the press,

[1] Friedrich, III. i. p. 244. Cf. *Revue internationale de Théologie*, 1903.

notwithstanding the ordinance of secrecy. But even before they appeared measures had been taken by the authorities, who fully realised the importance of the press. It was not known till after the Council was over that four of the fathers—fervent Infallibilists—Dechamps, Senestrey, Mermillod, and Manning—had been absolved from the oath of secrecy in order that they might make communications to a number of laymen with a view to contradicting false and calumnious reports on the part of the opposition press. Manning's confidant was a Protestant, the diplomatist Mr. Odo Russell, who was the English agent in Rome. Russell passed on Manning's information to Lord Clarendon, the Foreign Secretary, and he helped Manning by reporting to him all he could discover about the proceedings of the opposition. Russell was of considerable help in averting the danger of diplomatic intervention, and Purcell, the biographer of Manning, goes so far as to describe him as a human agent for aiding in carrying through the new dogma.[1]

On New Year's Day the Pope held his usual reception of the diplomatists, and he sought to assure them that nothing the Council would do would affect the Church's relations with the governments of Europe. "A great noise", he said, "was made about the *Syllabus*, but the ecclesiastical world has now acquiesced in its principles. It will be just the same with the decrees of the Council." In this prophecy he was perfectly right. The words show that Pius was quite confident as to the result. And Odo Russell observes that in Rome people generally mocked the

[1] Purcell, *Manning*, ii. pp. 435, 436.

naïveté of Cardinal Schwarzenberg and Bishop Dupanloup, who imagined for a moment they could oppose the Holy See; and records that Antonelli remarked, speaking of Dupanloup's futile excitations, that the *furia francese* was often forced to abate itself in Rome.[1] "The Jesuits", observes Russell, "are men of the world, and they do not usually undertake things they cannot carry through; for years they have been sounding the spirit of the Catholic populations and of the clergy, and they know perfectly well how far they can count on the superstition of the former and the servility and stupidity of the latter."[2] But the minority did not look on the situation with such a discerning eye; they thought they had to do, not with the world, but with the Church, and were not prepared for intrigues. The remark of Antonelli is one of the indications that the fate of the minority had been decided, and it was only for reasons of policy that the struggle of the parties was allowed to protract itself unmeaningly for six months.

Meanwhile the *Schema de fide*, on which the preparatory committee had been laboriously engaged for two years before, was submitted to the Council at the Congregation of December 28. It was hoped it would pass without any discussion, for the Pope was very anxious that it should be ready for formal promulgation on January 6, the date fixed for the Second Public Session.

It is said, and this has not been contradicted, that the schema was the work of the Jesuits Schrader and Franzelin. It was an enormously long document,

[1] Friedrich, III. ii. pp. 601-2; III. i. p. 268.
[2] Friedrich, III. i. pp. 268-9.

dealing with a number of heresies, and with the general question of the sources of divine revelation, and the meaning of tradition. It is quite unnecessary to touch upon its details. But though no time had been allowed to the fathers to study its details seriously, it was not to pass without criticism. Cardinal Rauscher opened the discussion, and proposed the rejection of the scheme.[1] Bishop Kenrick of St. Louis followed to the same effect. Then came Tizzani, a blind man, Archbishop of Nisibio, who condemned the document as mere words, *verba verba nil nisi verba*, and contrasted the brevity of the decrees of former Councils.[2] But the speech of the day was made by Connolly, the Archbishop of Halifax, who concluded with words that ran through Rome like wildfire: *Hoc schema non esse reformandum censeo cum honore sepeliendum.*[3] Cardinal Bilio, president of the Committee that was responsible for this precious document, hung his head and looked deeply dejected.[4] The majority were much disconcerted, but when the members of the minority left the hall in high satisfaction and naïvely began to praise the freedom of the Council, the majority took full advantage of this, and made the proceedings which had vexed them the text for proving to the world how free the Council was. It must be remembered that two-thirds of the Assembly could not hear what the outspoken critics said.

The debate was resumed on December 30, and was marked by the speech of Bishop Strossmayer

[1] Wolfsgruber, *Cardinal Rauscher*, p. 430.
[2] Friedrich, III. i. p. 323.
[3] Friedrich, III. i. pp. 324 ff.
[4] Cf. Icard, *Journal*, p. 193.

(of Diakovar in Bosnia).[1] He began to criticise the superscription of the scheme, "Pius, bishop, servant of the servants of God, with the approval of the Council", as against tradition and unsuitable to the decree of an Ecumenical Council, but he was interrupted by Cardinal Capalti, who pointed out that the superscription formula was fixed by the order of business as laid down in the Papal Brief and could not be discussed. Strossmayer replied that he would say with Bossuet, rather let my tongue be dried up than that I should attack the true rights of the Holy See—and descended from the tribune.

In support of Capalti and the presidents, it may be said that the order of business dictated by the Pope had been accepted by the Council and Congregations, and on that basis had already been held. But, on the other hand, there had been no opportunity before of discussing or protesting against the order of business. In any case the Capalti incident displayed the weakness of the minority. A strong and determined party would have seized the opportunity for a vigorous and combined protest. Many of them, no doubt, did not know what was going on. But afterwards, if they had had any discernment, they would have seen that their further presence at Rome was futile and undignified and would have left the Council. For the Capalti incident made it clear that the Council was based on a *petitio principii*. For the acceptance of the superscription was an acceptance of the principle that the Pope can alone define and is a legislator in dogma. What was the object, then, of continuing the fight for months

[1] *Acta Congr. gener.* ii. pp. 43 ff.; Icard, *Journal*, p. 193.

against Infallibility? A French journalist observed: "It was a true master stroke to set the Papal Infallibility in operation before it is proclaimed as a dogma". But the minority were blind, and praised Strossmayer as a second St. Bernard.

These proceedings—for more speakers were announced and the debate was continued on subsequent days—showed that the *Schema de fide* could not be proclaimed on January 6. The Pope saw it would be impolitic to intervene to cut short the discussion; it was expedient to let the bishops speak as much as they chose, and maintain the semblance of complete freedom. It was therefore necessary to invent something else for the Public Session of January 6. The directors of the Council resorted to an extraordinary expedient for occupying this Assembly. Each of the members present pledged himself to the Confession of Faith of the Council of Trent—the same pledge which he had taken when he was ordained; it was not taken to the Pope. Such a proceeding was entirely alien to the business and purpose of a Council, and caused no little disgust among the opposition.

In the meantime the promoters of Infallibility were devising how to bring this supreme question forward. Bishop Martin besought the Pope to have it proposed. Pius required in support of such a petition the names of at least 400 bishops, and Martin immediately set to work. The petition was prepared chiefly by him, Manning, and Dechamps. By January 2 it was printed, revised, and had fifteen signatures, and was ready to be sent to the members of the majority. The minority knew nothing about this movement till after the address was printed in *The Vatican* (Manning's paper) on the 15th and in more complete form on the 22nd January. The address obtained 410 names. At the same time, from the 6th to 16th, a sermon was preached every day in St. Andrea della Valle in favour of Infallibility. Bishop Mermillod outdid all the other preachers; his expressions were so strong that even the ultramontane press forbore to print his sermon. His subject was the three Bethlehems; and the three Bethlehems were the manger, the tabernacle, and the Vatican. "If you knock at the Vatican, who comes out? Christ and the gospel." Bishop Haynald asked him afterwards: "In which storey of the Vatican does Christ reside?" Mermillod answered quite good-humouredly: "I did not take a note of the number".[1]

On the same day on which this sermon was preached (January 9) Pius IX. received an audience of 1500 persons, and delivered a discourse in which he referred to the minority as *duces caecorum*.[2]

Pius also did something publicly for Infallibility. On January 5 he issued a brief to J. Jacques, a Redemptorist, who had written a book explaining Liguori's doctrine of Pope and Council. Pius said the book was not only good but opportune, on account of the Council now sitting, and would help to dissipate sophisms which were propagated under the semblance of a new philosophy. Thus the Pope, by this means, recommended Liguori to the Council.

Some prominent members of the minority held an international meeting, as it was called, on January 8,

[1] Friedrich, III. i. pp. 387-9.
[2] Friedrich, III. i. p. 390; his *Documenta*, i. p. 185.

and decided to draw up manifestoes, in the form of addresses to the Pope, against Infallibility. Several petitions resulted: one from the German and Austrian members; another from thirty French members, to which were added all the Portuguese names, some Armenians, and others; a third from the American, English, and Irish bishops, twenty-seven signatures; a fourth from sixteen Orientals; and a fifth from seven Italians. These extra-conciliar movements occupied the chief attention of the fathers now, and weakened the interest in the Congregations. The minority went on making tiresome speeches, for so long as the fate of the *Schema de fide* was not decided they persisted in talking, although they knew now that it was a subordinate matter. At the end of the Congregation on January 10 the President declared the debate closed, and the Scheme was referred to the dogmatic committee for correction. Meanwhile schemes on the subject of Church discipline would be brought forward at next Congregation.

The French bishops had already in preparation a memorial on ecclesiastical discipline and organisation, written by the Archbishop of Paris, and on January 13 they determined to hand it in to the Committee for Proposals. Among the *vota* of the French were that Ecumenical Councils should be more frequently held, also plenary and provincial Councils to which the Roman Congregation should not have the right of making additions unless submitted to and approved by the members; that the bishops should have a larger right to grant dispensations; that the Rules of the *Index Librorum Pro-*

hibitorum should be reformed, as they were useless and impracticable nowadays; that the Breviary with its apocryphal stories and obscure hymns should be corrected; and that the diffusion of pious pictures, miraculous legends, and introduction to new cults should be checked.[1] There was consternation in the Vatican when the tenor of this document was known, and two Dominican monks of the Inquisition paid a visit to Cardinal Hohenlohe to request him to use his influence with the German bishops not to send in such unsuitable propositions. "It is frightful," they said. "What will become of Rome? These bishops are working for a decentralisation of the Church."[2] They did not go to the right person, but in any case the Germans had already prepared a document of the same kind, which had been in preparation since the meeting of bishops at Fulda. The German propositions also tended to decentralisation, to securing and increasing the powers of the bishops, and included the revision of the rules of the Index, and of the Breviary, and a revised Corpus of the canon law.

The Roman Cardinals and members of the Roman Congregations were terribly alarmed at such demands. If dispensations and everything are taken out of the hands of Rome, they said, on what are we going to live?

The schemes which were proposed to the Congregation on January 14 tended in exactly the opposite direction. They were two—one on the bishops and synods, and one on the procedure in case of vacant sees. They aimed at securing greater centralisation

[1] *Collectio Lacensis*, p. 832. [2] Nielsen, ii. p. 331.

and stricter dependence of the bishops on Rome. In the debate on this and the following day, speakers insisted on the complete omission in the schemes of any reference to the rights of the bishops. The Pope was greatly put out by these discussions, and his anger vented itself on the presidents. But the debate continued through many meetings till January 25, when both schemes were withdrawn and referred for revision in Committee.

During these weeks lively war was carried on outside Rome; pamphlets and brochures were flying. The first bolt that caused great excitement at Rome was a letter of the Oratorian, Père Gratry, to Bishop Dechamps.[1] It was a drastic historical criticism on the doctrine of Infallibility, and professed to be an attack upon a "school of errors and lies". "Does God need your lies?" the writer asked.[2] He laid most stress on the notorious case of Pope Honorius, the main stumbling-block to adherents of Infallibility who take any account of historical facts.[3] This case alone, according to Gratry, decides the question.[4] On January 22 the Pope issued a Brief to the Abbé Ségur, which, if not caused by Gratry's letter, was a reply to it. "Is it so surprising", asked the Holy Father, "if the forces of hell, which have been once

[1] *L'évêque d'Orléans et Mgr. de Malines, Première lettre à Mgr. Dechamps*, 1870. There were four. Cf. Friedrich, *Döllinger*, iii. p. 521. Döllinger helped Gratry in his letters.

[2] *Première lettre*, p. 2. Cf. Frommann, pp. 66-71.

[3] *Première lettre*, pp. 15 ff. Cf. pp. 36, 37. Cf. Friedrich, III. i. pp. 480-82.

[4] Honorius I. (625–38) supported the monothelite heresy. It is important to note that the Council of Constantinople condemned him in 680, and in the oath taken by every new Pope from the eighth to the eleventh century, he was duly anathematised.

more vanquished by the assembling of the whole Church, should pull all their strength together to fight against the Council? Godless men are laying snares to postpone as long as possible the deadly stroke which in the end they will not escape."[1]

The petition in favour of Infallibility was published in the paper of the party, before the text appeared, in the Augsburg *Allgemeine Zeitung* on January 16. Five days later an article on the subject appeared in the same journal by Döllinger, entitled "Einige Worte".[2] In breaking silence at this juncture, Döllinger seems to have been prompted by a letter which he had just received from Arnim, the ambassador of the North German Federation at Rome. "The longer the bishops remain away from home", wrote Arnim, "and are exposed to the influence of the Roman spirit, the more pliable will they become. They are all excellent men, but they have lost the great ideas of the Church. Two months more at Rome, and there will be complete concord. The fault is largely due to the lifelessness of the Catholic world in Germany. It seems to me of the greatest importance to call public attention to the state of things, in order to organise a manifestation of opinion which will reach as far as Rome, and which should particularly be based on the principle that the Catholic world in Germany cannot possibly be induced to receive laws from 500 Italians, of whom 300 are parasites of the Pope."[3]

The publication of the Infallibility petition gave

[1] Friedrich, III. i. pp. 483-4; Friedenberg, *Aktenstücke*, pp. 489 ff.
[2] Friedrich, III. i. pp. 493-500.
[3] *Collectio Lacensis*, pp. 1471 c, ff.; Quirinus, p. 128.

Döllinger an opportunity to attempt to influence public opinion in Arnim's sense. His criticism was unsparing. He examined particularly certain assertions of the petition about the Council of Lyons (1274) and the Council of Florence (1439).[1] I will quote only the conclusion, in order to show the tone of a pronouncement which caused unspeakable fury in Rome. "The petition", he says, "is at pains to show that the promulgation of the new article of faith is just now opportune, or rather urgently necessary, because some persons who profess to be Catholics have recently disputed this opinion of Papal Infallibility. What the petition says, or assumes as known in Rome, on this head amounts to this: Abstractly, it would not have been necessary to augment the number of dogmas by a new one, but the situation has so developed that this can no longer be evaded. Years ago, the Jesuit Order, supported by followers of the same views, began an agitation in favour of the proposed dogma simultaneously in Italy, France, Germany and England. The chief organ of the Jesuits, the *Civiltà*, has designated it as the principal task of the Council to bestow upon the expectant world the article of faith which is still lacking; their publications at Maria Laach and in Vienna have ventilated the same theme untiringly. Those who disagree ought, they think, to have maintained a respectful silence in the presence of this agitation and to allow the arguments of their numerous writings to pass without criticism. Unfortunately this has not been the case. Some men have had the unheard of auda-

[1] Friedrich, III. i. pp. 495-6.

city to break that sacred silence and to express a different opinion. This offence can only be atoned for by an addition to the creed, a change in the catechism and all religious books."[1]

The article was an event; it created an uproar in the precincts of the Council. Döllinger, who bore the reputation in all lands of being the first theologian of the day—Döllinger *locutus est!* He had spoken, and the strength of his language surpassed expectation. It was a drastic exposure of the theological knowledge of the 369 bishops who had already signed. No one at Rome was more furious than Manning.[2] The order which forbade anyone to discuss Infallibility during the Council, within the Roman State, in a public print was now felt to be embarrassing by the promoters of the dogma, and on February 1 the Pope gave the Jesuit editors of the *Civiltà* a dispensation from this prohibition, so that they could print an article against Döllinger. Döllinger's criticism, however, was far from pleasing all the minority. There was naturally in parts of it a strong resemblance to *Janus*, and the bishops of the minority were strongly averse to identifying themselves with the attitude of Janus, though they agreed with it partly. They all entertained a violent dislike to the *Augsburger allgemeine Zeitung*, and were vexed that Döllinger should have contributed his paper to it. Ketteler was especially indignant, and was very anxious to get up a manifesto against Döllinger.[3]

[1] *Allgemeine Zeitung*, January 21; Friedrich, III. i. pp. 499-500; Friedenberg, pp. 495 ff.

[2] Purcell, *Life of Cardinal Manning*, ii. p. 433.

[3] Friedrich, III. i. pp. 504-6, 522-6; III. ii. pp. 588-90.

There were several points on which they could have disavowed agreement—for instance, the ecumenical character of the Council of Florence, which Döllinger denied, but Hefele and Strossmayer upheld.[1] But the proposal was not accepted.

It was while indignation with Döllinger's step was still fresh that the address of the minority against Infallibility was presented to the Pope, and a worse moment could not have been chosen for handing in an unwelcome petition. The Pope said it must be sent to the Committee of Proposals, for he did not interfere with the Council. It was not pleasing to him to learn that on January 27 Munich honoured Döllinger by making him an Ehrenburger, or honorary citizen.[2]

I may close this lecture with the incident of Audu, the Patriarch of Babylon.[3] On January 25, the last day of the debates on the schemes concerning Church discipline, the Patriarch had complained of the efforts of Rome to interfere with the ancient customs of the Church. The Pope, in fact, had in the previous September sent a Constitution *cum ecclesiastica disciplina* to the Chaldeans, which divested their Patriarch of important rights. Audu's speech was an appeal from the Pope to the Council. Pius IX. was indignant beyond measure. The same evening a Roman prelate summoned the Patriarch to appear before the Pope next morning, and he came without an interpreter, since a certain Valerga,

[1] Friedrich, III. i. pp. 503, 506-7, 543.

[2] *Allgemeine Zeitung*, January 28 (Supplement); Friedenberg, *Sammlung der Aktenstücke*, pp. 121 ff. Döllinger refused this honour.

[3] Friedrich, iii. p. 508; Quirinus, pp. 174-5.

whom the Propaganda had appointed to Latinise the East, would act as such. The Patriarch Audu went and found the Pope trembling with anger. Pius exclaimed: "So you are the stiff-necked troublesome man who has been vexing me so long. Your disobedience will have to bend before me." After many reproaches about the speech he had delivered the day before, the Pope placed two papers before him, one being a resignation of the Patriarchate, the other a nomination of two bishops whom the Pope had chosen for the Chaldeans, and whom the Patriarch and his Church had refused to accept. Audu, who was nearly eighty years old, prayed for a postponement of three or at least two days for consideration. The Pope refused—you must sign at once. The Patriarch took the pen and began, then stopped, saying the pen would not write. The Pope supplied a penknife, Valerga pared the pen, and the Patriarch wrote—the effect of the signatures being that he would consecrate the two priests as bishops within two hours or resign.[1] He did consecrate them, but he confided the whole transaction to one of his Oriental colleagues; it was known throughout Rome and created a great impression.[2] Darboy said: "It is simply a robber synod. What is to be thought of its freedom, men asked, if a bishop is liable to be called to account for his speech by the Pope and perhaps even punished?"[3]

[1] *Giornale di Roma*, February 1, 1870.

[2] Friedrich, *Tagebuch*, pp. 140 ff.; *Stimmen aus der kath. Kirche*, ii. pp. 180 ff.; Ollivier, *L'Église et l'État*, ii. p. 185; Quirinus, p. 138; Friedrich, *Geschichte*, iii. p. 508.

[3] Cf. Friedrich, i. pp. 435-7; Friedenberg, *Aktenstücke*, pp. 257 ff.; *Ce qui se passe au Concile*, p. 17; *La vérité sur Mgr. Darboy*, p. 37.

V

THE VATICAN COUNCIL

The bishops who formed the minority of the Council, although to some extent conscious already of the undignified, helpless, and illogical position which they occupied, had not the courage or unanimity to take a decisive step, and still struggled on, hoping to gain succour partly from public opinion outside, influenced by the authority of men like Döllinger, and partly from diplomatic intervention. From Prussia nothing was to be hoped; Bismarck declined to take any interest in the Council;[1] in his despatch of January 5 to the Prussian envoy at Rome he explained at length that the decrees of the Council could not affect Prussia. "We do not in the least require an assurance on the Pope's part that the relations of the Curia to the governments shall not be altered by the Conciliar decrees."[2] And later, on March 13, he wrote in the same sense; the government would give its moral support to a firm attitude on the part of the North German bishops; but it was for them to act, not for the government.[3] It was on the attitude of France that the hopes of the minority chiefly de-

[1] Meglia to Antonelli, July 8, 1869.

[2] *Collectio Lacensis*, 1202 d, ff., 1206 a, ff.; Cecconi, Doc. clxxx.

[3] *Collectio Lacensis*, p. 1608 a.

pended; and French diplomacy at this moment gave some false grounds for hope.[1] On January 2 Napoleon had resorted to a ministry under the presidency of Émile Ollivier, a ministry whose members were far from holding the same views on ecclesiastical affairs.[2] Daru was the Foreign Minister; he was a friend of Dupanloup, and strongly adverse to Infallibility. Whatever instructions Daru wrote to Banneville,[3] the envoy at Rome, and whatever words he uttered on the question of the Council, Ollivier, a man full of confidence in his own omniscience, disavowed, and thus lowered the respect for the French government at the Vatican.[4] When the preparation of the petition for Infallibility was known at Paris, Daru sent an instruction to Banneville, expressing views which he desired to be laid before Antonelli. He pointed out the policy of the Holy See was making the situation difficult for the French government, which would have to explain in the Chamber the retention of the French troops; and he complained of the methods by which the freedom of the bishops had been curtailed in a manner without precedent. The next day, Daru

[1] The serious matter for the minority was that Ollivier was opposed to all interference. He defended his action by maintaining that it is true and sound policy in our time to respect religious liberty fully, and, moreover, that it would have been undignified on the part of France to offer ineffectual remonstrance. But he forgets that French troops were then supporting Pius IX. in interfering with liberty. Napoleon III. said to Odo Russell: "Je crois, et j'ai toujours cru, que l'occupation de Rome sera la faute de ma règne". No truer words were ever spoken. They will be the final verdict of history.

[2] Ollivier, *L'Église et l'État*, ii. p. 33; *Revue des Deux Mondes*, March 1, 1924.

[3] *Collectio Lacensis*, pp. 1553 ff.; Friedrich, III. ii. p. 737; Paul, *Letters of Lord Acton*, xli.

[4] Ollivier, *L'Empire libéral*, ii. pp. 210-39; Friedenberg, pp. 521 ff.; Ollivier, *L'Église et l'État*, ii. p. 126.

wrote in much stronger terms to his friend Du Boys, the vicar-general of Dupanloup. "They can hardly be blind enough", he said, "to suppose that we will leave our troops there a single day, once they proclaim the dogma of Infallibility. . . . Public opinion in France will be too strong."[1] But Banneville did not move in the sense of Daru's instructions; and this was due to the fact that the premier Ollivier was working behind Daru's back, and indirectly assuring the Vatican that in the opinion of the government intervention was unreasonable and the Council was perfectly free.[2] The Pope and his advisers knew that there was nothing to fear for the present, and some ambiguous menaces on the part of Austria were equally without result.[3] The Pope used to say: "I cannot help laughing at these governments".

Speaking in the senate on the subject, Count Daru had appealed to the great principles of 1789. Now in the preceding October the editor of the *Univers* had asserted that men like Döllinger, Maret, Montalembert[4] wanted an '89 for the Church; and the *Civiltà*, in its recent article against Döllinger, imputed to him the design of substituting, instead of the monarchy instituted by God, a modern constitutional régime. These observations made a great impression on Pius IX., and he became convinced that the liberal Catholics and all the opponents of Infallibility

[1] Friedenberg, p. 136. The second sentence is a paraphrase. Cf. Friedrich, III. ii. pp. 818-19.

[2] Ollivier, ii. pp. 133-7; *Collectio Lacensis*, pp. 1559-60; Friedenberg, III. ii. pp. 736-9.

[3] *Collectio Lacensis*, pp. 1577 a, 1578 c, d, 1579 a, 1581 b, 1593 a, ff., 1602 c, ff. On Bismarck's attitude cf. the *Collectio*, pp. 1608-10.

[4] Contrast Pelletier, *Dupanloup*, pp. 94 ff.

were ecclesiastical revolutionaries and desired a 1789 for the Church. And so he seized an early opportunity of branding the year 1789. On the 17th of February he opened an exhibition of art, and observed in the course of his address: "It is not true that, as some say, our religion requires a year '89; that is a blasphemy, borrowed from a great Italian demagogue".[1] Nobody doubted that in these words the Pope was attacking the minority. Just after this utterance the *Moniteur Universel*[2] arrived from Paris, containing an article on the Council of which Darboy afterwards acknowledged himself the author.[3] It showed unsparingly how the members had found at Rome a Council already constituted by theologians and canonists who had been selected on exclusive principles and had framed resolutions which the bishops were expected to sanction.[4] The order of procedure had been imposed on them, they had not elected a single officer; and the arrangements were made in order, as Veuillot said, to deprive the bishops of the freedom to do wrong. "The Italian bishops and apostolic vicars are masters of the Council and of the votes, and the Roman Curia can crush the minority by numbers, although the minority represent a population of 90 millions, *i.e.* about half the Catholic world."[5]

In the meantime a scheme had been proposed to the Council for introducing a short catechism that should be used universally in all countries, supersed-

[1] Cf. Nielsen, ii. p. 340.

[2] Article of February 14, 1870; Quirinus, p. 227; Friedrich, *Tagebuch*, p. 191; Veuillot, *Rome pendant le Concile*, i. p. 275.

[3] Ollivier, *L'Église et l'État au Concile*, ii. p. 91; his *Empire libéral*, xiii. p. 148. Cf. Cornu, *Mgr. Freppel*, p. 168.

[4] Ollivier, *L'Église*, ii. p. 272; Friedrich, *Geschichte*, iii. p. 899, and his *Tagebuch*, p. 380.

[5] *Collectio Lacensis*, p. 1567.

ing all local or national catechisms.[1] The intention of Rome was that it should be a vehicle for introducing Infallibility. Like other schemes, this, too, was returned to the Committee for revision on February 22, and at the same time the Council was informed that the Pope had decided on a new order of procedure, in order to accelerate the work of the Council, and this was read out. Members were required henceforward to send in writing their objections to the proposals laid before Council, and they must propose amendments for all classes or paragraphs they objected to. The committee was to revise the scheme with all these criticisms before them, and then bring it forward again, on which the real discussion was to be held. In case *ten* members proposed to close the debate and the majority agreed, the closure was to be enforced. At the voting a qualified affirmative *placet iuxta modum* might be given, but the condition was to be handed in in writing.

The minority were dismayed by the new ordinance, for it placed the liberty of discussion entirely in the hands of the majority, and deprived the Council of the small appearance of freedom it possessed. It was felt by a great many bishops that the only dignified and reasonable thing to do was to leave Rome, but they had not the resolution, and they still secretly hoped something would be done by the French government.[2] A strong protest was drawn up and

[1] Granderath, ii. pp. 257-77.

[2] Cf. Bourgeois and Clermont, *Rome et Napoléon III*, 1849–70. Bourgeois describes the negotiations which took place between 1868 and August 1870, with a view to the formation of a Triple Alliance between Austria, France, and Italy against the growing power of Prussia. He proves with the utmost clearness that the main obstacle

signed by more than a hundred bishops, pointing out the anomalies and injustice of the new arrangements, but they did not say that unless it were withdrawn they would retire from the Council, and it had no effect. But this protest forms in itself a striking criticism on the character of the Assembly. It illustrates the fact that the Vatican Council was indeed a very large gathering, but a gathering whose powers and competence were so indeterminate that it is difficult to see in what sense it can be called a Council. The protest and the circumstances which evoked it show that it was quite unsettled what were the relations of the Council to the Pope; whether the Assembly was merely advisory or had a decisive voice. It was not settled whether a simple majority was sufficient to decide whether a dogmatic decree would be invalid against which a minority voted, or how large a majority must be in order to make it invalid. Some held one opinion, some another; but nothing had been definitely and bindingly laid down, and the whole proceedings were chaotic, the only principal order being the Pope's despotic will.

Meanwhile the *Schema de Ecclesia* had become known at Paris.[1] Even Ollivier admitted that its canons were dangerous, since they involved the indirect power of the State over the Church. Daru drew up a strongly worded despatch to Antonelli, in which he referred to political complications which

to the conclusion of that Triple Alliance was the French occupation of Rome. Cf. Mazziotti's *Napoleone III e l' Italia*. Mazziotti and Bourgeois are in substantial agreement that French bayonets in Rome formed the main reason why Napoleon III. had to face Prussia alone.

[1] Granderath, ii. pp. 316 ff.

might involve military operations on the Rhine and necessitate the withdrawal of the French division from Roman territory.[1] It was despatched on February 20: next day there was a council of ministers, and Daru mentioned that he had sent it. His colleagues demanded to hear it, and decided that it must be revised. A telegram was sent to Banneville to keep it back, and Ollivier and Daru together watered it down, omitting everything in the nature of a menace; another cabinet council expurgated it still more; so that it had no effect except doubtless to cause Antonelli to smile.[2] The political situation in Europe was for the moment favourable to Rome. The war was already on the horizon. The Archduke Albrecht was in Paris at this time; he was the head and heart of the war party in Austria, who were thirsting for revenge on Prussia. The overthrow of the ministry of Prince Hohenlohe in Bavaria, and also of the ministry in Würtemberg, were both victories for the anti-Prussian party in South Germany and also for the ultramontanes. France saw in these events a favourable situation for intervention, to prevent in time the realisation of Prussian schemes for the unification of Germany. It was, therefore, in the eyes of the French ministry, of great importance to keep on good terms with Rome, with a view to ultramontane support both at home and in South Germany.

One of the curious things about this Council was

[1] Ollivier, ii. p. 87.

[2] Ollivier, ii. pp. 126 ff.; *Collectio Lacensis*, pp. 1553 ff. Cf. Ollivier, ii. pp. 130 ff.; *Collectio Lacensis*, p. 1578 ff. Antonelli's letter to the nuncio is in the *Collectio*, pp. 1555 ff.

that while all the members knew that the definition of Infallibility was its principal object, a large number of the minority never seemed able to realise that it would come to pass, and their surprise was great when on the 7th and 8th March the apostolic messengers distributed at their houses the text of an additional chapter to the *Schema de Ecclesia*, containing a definition of Infallibility—in answer, as a covering letter said, to the petition of a large number of fathers. Criticisms were to be sent in within ten days. It was hoped that the dogma would be proclaimed on the 19th of March, the feast of St. Joseph. The energy of the minority was able, however, to hinder this precipitation. Four American bishops wrote, protesting that if it were hurried they would leave Rome, and explain the whole circumstances to the Catholics of the United States.[1] Dupanloup wrote to Cardinal de Angelis, threatening to proclaim to the world how dogmas were manufactured in Rome.[2] The Pope and the Presidents of the Assembly saw that it would not do to push the matter as hastily as the extreme enthusiasts desired, and the plan was abandoned.[3] A pasquinade was placarded in Rome at the Pope's expense:

> Eve ate the apple and made Adam eat,
> Christ made himself a man, thus man to save;
> Christ's vicar, Pius, wrought another feat,
> Made himself God, to render man a slave.

Two weighty utterances about the proceedings of the Council appeared at this time. One was a

[1] *Collectio Lacensis*, pp. 975 c, ff.
[2] *Diarium, Quae de definitione Infallibilitatis acta sunt*, n. 25.
[3] *Diarium*, n. 29.

letter of Newman to Ullathorne, Bishop of Birmingham, of which numerous copies were circulated, expressing grief and dismay at the policy of the ultramontane party and the majority. He urges the absence of all need for defining the dogma, which might cause no difficulty to him and others personally, but will cause pains of conscience to multitudes. "What have we done to be treated as the faithful have never been treated before? When has a definition of doctrine *de fide* been a luxury of devotion and not a stern painful necessity?"[1] But a far greater sensation was made by the last pronouncement of Montalembert. He had been long urged to raise his voice. He wrote a letter to Döllinger on February 28; it appeared in the *Gazette de France* on March 7;[2] he died on the 13th. He had been accused of inconsistency. "I venture to assert", he replied, "that not a word will be found in my speech of 1847, or in any of my speeches or writings, to support the doctrines or pretensions of the ultramontanism of to-day. I once said 'Gallicanism is dead, because it made itself the servant of the state, and you have only to bury it'. That, I think, was true then. It was dead, but it has risen again. What is the cause of its resurrection? I will tell you. It is due to the prodigal encouragement of extreme doctrines in the Pontificate of Pius IX., doctrines which insult both sane common-sense and the honour of the human race, doctrines of which there was not a shadow in the reign of Louis Philippe. How could we then foresee

[1] Ward, *Life of John Henry Cardinal Newman*, ii. p. 288; *Collectio Lacensis*, pp. 1513 ff.; Icard, *Journal*, pp. 278-9.

[2] *Collectio Lacensis*, pp. 1385 a, ff.; Friedrich, iii. pp. 701, 704.

the triumph of those lay theologians of absolutism, who have offered up justice and truth, reason and history, in one great burnt offering to the *idol* which they set up in the *Vatican*? If the word idol seems too strong, you must censure the words which Archbishop Sibour wrote to me in 1853: 'The new ultramontane school leads us to a double idolatry—the idolatry of secular and the idolatry of spiritual power'."[1]

The idol in the Vatican was deeply outraged by the attack of the great Liberal Catholic. Immediately after he had heard the news of Montalembert's death he gave an audience to 300 persons, and pronounced this epitaph: "A Catholic has just died who performed services for the Church. He has written a letter which I have read. I know not what he said in the hour of his death; but I do know this man had one great enemy—pride. He was a liberal Catholic, that is, he was a half-Catholic. Yes, the liberal Catholics are only half-Catholics."[2] Thus Pius expressed his resentment. A funeral service had been prepared at Rome in the Frenchman's honour, for he had been created a Roma Patricius, in recognition of his services, long ago by the Pope, and it was customary to hold a service for deceased Patricii in the Church of Ara Coeli; but at the last moment the ceremony was forbidden.[3]

[1] *Collectio Lacensis*, p. 1385 a. Cf. Ollivier, *L'Église et l'État*, ii. p. 171, and his *L'Empire libéral*, xiii. pp. 142 ff.

[2] *Univers*, March 14, 1870. Printed in Ollivier, *L'Église et l'État*, ii. p. 175. Cf. Baunard, *Cardinal Pie*, ii. p. 392; Maynard, *Dupanloup*, p. 259; *Wie es auf dem Concil zugeht*, p. 195.

[3] *Univers*, March 21, 1870. Printed in Friedenberg, *Sammlung*, p. 109.

Simultaneously with the news of the French leader's death, there arrived at Rome a number of the *Allgemeine Zeitung* containing an article by Döllinger mercilessly criticising the new regulation of procedure, in the light of the *sententia communis* of the Church, and insisting that unanimity at Councils had always been recognised as a *sine qua non* for Catholic doctrine.[1] It made a great impression even on members of the minority like Ketteler who disapproved of *Janus* and Döllinger's school. It was suspected, however, that Ketteler was not altogether sincere, that he was pretending to act with the minority, but was playing a double game. I may read an extract from a recently published letter of Cardinal Hohenlohe to his brother:

> We are having a bad time now, especially here. Friedrich is a great stand-by for me, and in spite of all enmities I have been able to keep him by me. What indeed will be decided in the great question is by no means clear. Stupidity and fanaticism are dancing a tarantella together, accompanied by such discordant music that one can hardly see or hear. The Bishop of Mainz, I fear, is leading the German minority into a pitfall. He deceives these gentlemen by his abuse of Rome and so forth, and works against them behind their backs, and the excellent gentlemen take him at his word![2]

Again in a later letter (May 7, 1870):

> I go as little as possible to the meetings of the [Vatican] Council. . . . Ketteler persecutes Professor

[1] *Allgemeine Zeitung* (Augsburg), July 19, 1870; Friedrich, III. ii. pp. 720-29; Acton, *Sendschreiben*, p. 15.

[2] *Memoirs of Prince Hohenlohe*, vol. ii. p. 1.

Friedrich behind his back in the vilest fashion, as will be seen from the last pamphlet, in which he openly slanders him. But this prince of the Church is again foremost among the good German bishops, thanks to his manœuvring: the "noble Ketteler" one hears everywhere and so forth.[1]

The truth is that Ketteler hated the Döllinger school and took especial pains to separate himself from it in his opposition to the definition of Infallibility and to the procedure of the Council, which was perfectly genuine. He did not like to find himself in such company, fighting in the same cause.

The theologians of the majority set aside Döllinger's arguments by saying: "Döllinger is already a formal heretic, for he has appealed to public opinion". Senestrey, the Infallibilist Bishop of Regensburg, replied by forbidding all theological students of his diocese to attend Döllinger's lectures and imbibe erroneous and corrupting doctrines; and by writing a long article in a Regensburg paper, in which he showed to his own satisfaction that "Döllinger ist wissenschaftlich vernichtet" (annihilated by the arguments of his adversaries).

As I have already said, the hopes of the minority were depending on the possibility of inducing the powers to intervene, and the bishops of the French opposition directly addressed the Premier in a document which reached him about March 9, drawn up by the Archbishop of Paris. The argument of the paper was that Infallibility was a political question.

[1] *Memoirs of Prince Hohenlohe*, vol. ii. p. 10. Cf. *Historische Zeitschrift*, v. p. 571 (1908). Mirbt's article in the *Realenzyklopädie für protestantische Theologie u. Kirche*, xx. pp. 468 ff. (1908), deserves consultation.

"It is a true revolution to place the absolute government of consciences in Italian hands, under the name of personal, absolute, and separate Infallibility. France did not conclude the Concordat with the Church which will now be created. It is thus clear that Infallibility is not a dogmatic or speculative controversy, but touches the independence and tranquillity of the nations. And the new dogma has been demanded from a Council which is not free, and which is deeply divided. Can the government of France, without whose consent the bishops could not have come together and deliberated, take upon itself, in the eyes of the world and of history, the responsibility for a Council, which by its organisation, composition, and direction, by the principles which inspire it and by the passions which animate it, will, so far from producing the slightest good, let loose religious storms for long years to come? All legitimate means should be used to prorogue the Council. Send an extraordinary ambassador to explain reasons, and induce the other governments to do the same."[1]

Such were the representations of the minority. At the same time the French members of the majority sent the Bishop of Pondicherry to Paris to keep the ministry in the right way; while a middle party, of which the leader was Cardinal Bonnechose, and who considered the majority injudicious, sent a messenger in the person of Mgr. Forcade, Bishop of Nevers. At the same time Banneville was summoned to Paris (March 17) to give full explanations of the situation at Rome.

[1] *Collectio Lacensis*, p. 1551. Bury condenses considerably. Cf. p. 1567.

Ollivier was determined to do nothing decisive, but the government drafted a memorandum, repeating the mild warnings of Daru's previous despatch and not touching the question of Infallibility, which they had resolved to treat as outside the sphere of politics. Other governments to whom the memorandum was communicated supported it. Beust instructed the Austrian ambassador (Trautmannsdorff) to urge the same views on the Vatican vigorously.[1] Bavaria, England, Spain, and Portugal supported it too.[2] And Arnim, the ambassador of the North German League, recommended it strongly to the Vatican, observing that the German bishops coincided in the opinion of the French government as to the danger of the dogmatic decrees.[3] The despatch was delivered by Banneville when he returned to Rome on April 22. But in the meantime, on April 11, the Foreign Minister Daru resigned, Ollivier taking over his duties. The telegram which carried the news to Rome added the comment: "The Council is now free"; for Daru represented the adverse element in the ministry.[4] The ultramontanes counted on Ollivier, and at this moment they could put on the screw, for the elections were approaching, and the extreme Catholic party even hoped to obtain a guarantee from the government in regard to the Roman question, in return for a promise to support their policy in other matters. This, indeed, the govern-

[1] *Collectio Lacensis*, pp. 1570 ff., 1585 ff.

[2] *Ibid.* pp. 1572 ff.; Purcell, ii. p. 445.

[3] Baunard, *Cardinal Pie*, ii. p. 398; Lagrange, *Dupanloup*, iii. pp. 155 ff.; Veuillot, *Rome pendant le concile*, i. p. 462.

[4] Ollivier, ii. p. 225.

ment refused; but Ollivier's goodwill seemed assured. In these circumstances the Pope and Antonelli could afford to treat with neglect the French memorandum, which was a weak remonstrance,[1] backed by no menaces; and the ambassador was informed that such a document could not possibly be laid before the Council.

While this mild effort at diplomatic intervention was going on, the work of the Council was slowly proceeding. On March 18 the *Schema de fide* was brought forward in its revised form. The introduction now contained a characterisation of Protestantism as the root of all errors and evils in the world, first producing rationalism and indifference, and then leading on to the abyss of pantheism, materialism, and atheism, and annihilating the foundations of society. "As this godless pestilence (*pestis*) can range at large with impunity, many sons of the Church are necessarily infected by it." The inference was drawn as to the purpose of the Council. "We [the Pope] by our apostolic authority have summoned this ecumenical Council, in order, from our Cathedra, to prescribe and condemn these errors." If the minority accepted this they would acknowledge both the ecumenical character of the Council and the complete dependence of the Council on the Pope. As the text was circulated to all the members of the Council, about 700, it was impossible that the Protestants at Rome should not hear of the violent attack on Protestantism, and it was soon noised abroad.

The minority were in a dilemma at this juncture.

[1] So Ollivier owns, ii. p. 212.

They had denounced the new regulation of procedure. If they took part in the discussion on March 18, they would practically surrender their position, and acquiesce in what they condemned. They decided to participate, and their motion was, as the Archbishop of Paris explained, to avoid a scandal.[1] Strossmayer, who was the most courageous man at Rome, opposed this resolve as cowardly, and he determined to take the first opportunity to protest vigorously in the Congregation.[2] He spoke on the second day of the debate, March 22, and his action caused a stormy and scandalous scene.[3] He dealt with the attack on Protestantism, which he described as both untrue and uncharitable. It was not true to ascribe to Protestantism the growth of religious error. Many of the errors condemned in the decree were condemned and detested by Protestants as much as by Catholics; and where they err, they err in good faith. (He was interrupted by cries of "This is not the place to praise Protestants. Fie, down with the heretic!") Then he went on to attack the new procedure, and declared that the abrogation of the necessity of unanimity had destroyed the ecumenical character of the Council. The majority, apprehending the insinuation that on this principle Infallibility could not be proclaimed, jumped to their feet, raging furiously, and cried: "Down with him from the pulpit".[4] They thronged up and threatened him with violence. He descended protesting, and

[1] Acton, *Zur Geschichte des vatikan. Konzils*, p. 86.

[2] Friedrich, *Geschichte*, iii. p. 766.

[3] *Acta Congr. gener.* ii. pp. 43 ff.

[4] Acton, *Zur Geschichte des vatikan. Konzils*, p. 90; Friedrich, iii. pp. 773-9.

the meeting broke up in tumult.[1] Many of the minority thought that Strossmayer had gone much too far, but Dupanloup and some others supported him.[2] His words perhaps contributed to the result that the passage on Protestantism was revised, but this was chiefly due to the energetic action of Arnim, who, having assured himself that Protestantism was described as *pestis* in the decree, communicated with Berlin, and on March 25 was instructed to tell the Vatican that if the expression were retained it would probably influence the position of the representative of a Protestant king at Rome, for it was a grave insult to the Prussian king.[3] As a member of the German embassy said to some of the German bishops: "What would be thought if the Prussian king in a throne speech designated the Pope, in the words of Montalembert, as the idol in the Vatican?" Antonelli saw that it would be wise to yield. The objectionable preamble was re-written in the revised scheme, and the decree *de fide* was passed on April 24[4] in the third public session of the Council by a unanimous vote of 667 placets, the minority having determined, under the influence of Schwarzenberg, to yield, as the decree was really of minor importance. Strossmayer, and he alone, stayed away from the voting. This was the last act of the Council at which virtually all of the bishops assisted. But though the decree *de fide* was less thorny than the decree *de*

[1] *Acta Congr. gener.* ii. pp. 48 ff.; Acton, *History of Freedom*, pp. 541-2.

[2] Cf. *Diarium: Quae de definitione Infallibilitatis sunt*, n. 25.

[3] Hase, *Polemik*, pp. 40 ff.; his *Annalen meines Lebens*, pp. 216 ff.; Friedrich, iii. pp. 780-89.

[4] Cf. the two different forms in *Officielle Aktenstücke*, ii. pp. 129 ff.

ecclesia, it committed the minority to the positions against which they were contending.[1] At the end of the decree, the duty was laid down of obeying the constitutions and decrees in which not actually heretical opinions have been proscribed.[2] Many bishops were induced to swallow this by the assurance that it did not refer to questions of doctrine, and was a mere matter of discipline and obedience. But virtually, though not *totidem verbis*, the Council by passing this decree accepted Infallibility. As Lord Acton says: "In requiring submission to papal decrees on matters not articles of faith . . . they were investing with new authority the existing Bulls, and giving unqualified sanction to the Inquisition and the Index, to the murder of heretics and the deposing of kings".[3] "The Court of Rome became thenceforth reckless in its scorn of the opposition, and proceeded in the belief that there was no protest they would not forget, no principle they would not betray, rather than defy the Pope in his wrath."[4]

In the Congregation on April 29, at which the scheme of a catechism was again discussed, it was announced by Cardinal de St. Angelis that all schemes, both dogmatic and disciplinary, already prepared would be laid aside and the question of Infallibility would be taken up.[5] On the 6th of May a protest was sent in by the sixty-nine bishops of the opposition, objecting to the separation of the questions of the Primacy and the Infallibility from the

[1] *Collectio Lacensis*, p. 256.
[2] Quirinus, pp. 435 ff.; Acton, pp. 94 ff.
[3] Acton, *History of Freedom*, p. 534.
[4] *Ibid.* p. 544.
[5] Friedrich, III. ii. pp. 876-8.

rest of the whole body of doctrine *de ecclesia*. It contained complaints of what the Pope had done himself by allocutions and otherwise to put Infallibility in the foreground, and of the way in which the petitions of the minority had hitherto been treated. "This is not a petition, but a remonstrance against the mode of transacting business which is injurious both for the Church and the apostolic see."[1]

It was at this moment that there arrived at Rome a French pamphlet entitled *Ce qui se passe au Concile*, which described the history of the Council up to the middle of April, and showed that it was a mere caricature of an ecumenical Council.[2] The author used solely documents which had found their way into print, and the information supplied by ultramontane journals, especially the *Univers*. The book was promptly suppressed in Rome, but it was in everybody's hands. The antidote was presently supplied by a work by Cardoni proving Infallibility.

Cardoni was in a few days rewarded by being appointed Keeper of the Vatican Archives, instead of Thenier. The deposition of this learned scholar was a triumph for the Jesuits, whose enemy he was, and indirectly a slap in the face to the minority.[3] The Jesuits feared him because he had in his private possession documents which were compromising for their order, and they could not bear goodwill to the author of the biography of Clement XIV. During

[1] Friedrich, III. ii. pp. 877-8.

[2] Frommann, *Geschichte u. Kritik des vatikanischen Concils von 1869 u. 1870*, pp. 108, 128 ff., 206.

[3] Gisiger, *P. Theiner u. die Jesuiten* pp. 61 f.

the Council his private library had been the great stand-by to members of the opposition; for it was the only considerable theological library at Rome that contained the new literature; and it also contained the procedure of the Council of Trent, which Thenier, as Keeper of the Archives, had been forbidden to show to the bishops. Already in March an attack had been made on Thenier; the Jesuits told the Pope that he had betrayed his trust. The Pope summoned him and charged him with having admitted Lord Acton into the Archives and thus committed treachery of the worst kind. Thenier swore solemnly that the charge was untrue. The Pope was satisfied for the time, enjoined on Thenier to say nothing to Lord Acton, and then reproached the librarian for his friendship with such men as Döllinger and Friedrich.[1] But afterwards a printed copy of the procedure of the Council of Trent was procured by Friedrich, though not from Thenier, and was shown by him to several German bishops. Strossmayer seems then to have obtained a copy from Thenier. But it came from his private library, not from the Vatican Archives. When this was known, the storm burst and Thenier had to surrender the keys.

Meanwhile on May 9 the members of the Council received notice that the beginning of the general debate was fixed for the 13th (the Pope's birthday), and at the same time the revised text of the eleventh chapter of the *Schema de ecclesia*, which concerned the Primacy, along with the supplementary canon on Infallibility which had been brought before the

[1] Friedrich, III. ii. pp. 1039-40.

Council on March 6 and had since been revised. In its new form the eleventh chapter consisted of four parts: (1) On the institution of the Apostolical primacy in the person of Peter; (2) on the continuance of the Primatus Petri in the Roman pontiffs; (3) on the power and nature of the primacy; and (4) on the Infallibility of the Roman pontiff.[1] Some of the criticisms of the minority had been taken into account by the Jesuits who revised the scheme, but there were no serious alterations. Monsigneur Pie, Bishop of Poitiers, opened the general debate on May 13, having had conversations immediately before with the Pope and with the Jesuits, Schrader and Franzelin. The calibre of the Bishop of Poitiers may be estimated by one of his arguments. The Apostle Peter, he said, had been crucified with his head downwards, so that his head bore his body;[2] even so the Pope is the head who bears up the Church which is the body; but evidently it is he who bears that is Infallible, and not that which is borne.[2] Next day the discussion began, and Manning treated the Assembly to his sophistical arguments for two hours.[3] In the course of the debate, which lasted about three weeks, the speeches of Darboy, Strossmayer, and of Connolly, Bishop of Halifax, seem to have been the most striking of those delivered by the opponents of the decree. Connolly had come to Rome believing in Infallibility, having never studied the evidence. He plunged into a study of

[1] *Collectio Lacensis*, pp. 269 ff.

[2] *Ibid.* p. 300 c; Quirinus, p. 412; Friedrich, iii. p. 982; Ollivier, ii. p. 279.

[3] *Acta*, iii. pp. 275 ff.

the question during the Council, and became convinced that the arguments were entirely against it.[1]

The general debate was closured on June 3, though many still desired to speak, and eighty French and German bishops signed a short protest against the closure, which, however, was ruled out of order, as the closuring was in accordance with the new regulation of business.[2]

The special debate, which was to consider the parts of the decree one by one, began on June 6. On the 18th they reached the section on Infallibility. As the president informed the Council that seventy-four members had announced their intention of speaking, it was hoped by the minority that the Council would have to be prorogued before the question came to a vote, as the heat was becoming intolerable; some members were falling ill, and all were exhausted. On the first day the Dominican Archbishop of Bologna, Cardinal Guidi, made a bold and dramatic speech, asserting that separate Personal Infallibility of the Pope was unknown till the fourteenth century, that even in Bellarmine's works there were passages inconsistent with it, and from him and Perrone it could be proved that the Pope had never condemned a heresy by his own authority.[3] This was too much for the Council, and the speaker was overwhelmed with words of abuse.[4] After a long interruption he resumed, and quoted St. Thomas Aquinas in his support. Few speeches

[1] *Acta*, iii. pp. 446 ff.

[2] Granderath, III. i. pp. 285-7; Friedrich, ii. pp. 392 ff., 399.

[3] Quirinus, pp. 671 f.; Pomponio Leto, pp. 279 f.; Friedrich, III. ii. p. 1109; *Acta*, iv. pp. 327 ff.

[4] Friedrich, III. ii. p. 1110.

at the Council produced a greater sensation than this.[1] The scene had an epilogue. When the Assembly broke up, Guidi was summoned to the presence of the Pope, who had been informed of the tenor of his discourse, and was received with the following words: "Well, Cardinal, you have just delivered an unworthy and heretical speech. You will return to Bologna, and doubtless make yourself useful to the Italian revolutionaries. Well, you will not return till you have signed a new confession of faith." The Cardinal replied the Pope must have been misinformed about his speech, and begged him to read it. He then briefly referred to his arguments and showed him that what he said was in accordance with scripture, the general teaching of the Church, and *tradition*. Here the Pope interrupted him with the words which became famous: "La Tradizione son' Io"—words which pregnantly express the ultramontane system.[2] Pius gave Guidi the choice of retracting or suspension. Guidi declined to retract.

[1] Friedrich, III. ii. p. 1112; Granderath, III. ii. p. 23.

[2] Nielsen, ii. p. 361; Friedrich, III. ii. pp. 1113-15; Acton, *Zur Gesch.* p. 112; Quirinus, p. 178; Frommann, p. 188. Cf. Mourret, *Le Concile du Vatican*, p. 299. Mourret gives Dupanloup's version of these famous words: "Des témoins de la tradition? Il n'y a qu'un. C'est moi." Cf. *Historische Zeitschrift*, v. p. 552 (1908); Granderath, III. ii. pp. 16-23; Martin, *Histoire de France*, vii. p. 146.

VI

THE DOCTRINE OF INFALLIBILITY

On the 2nd and 3rd of July the German and Austrian and the French members of the minority decided to abandon the policy of forcing a prorogation by protracting the debate, and declared their intention of speaking no more. If they had waited another day they might have come to a different resolve. The Curia and the leaders of the majority, who had better sources of information, were aware of the approach of the war, and were reckoning with it as a factor. The minority appear to have had no idea of its imminence. A French bishop on July 4 received a telegram from Paris: "Hold out yet a few days, Providence is sending an unexpected help".[1] This message meant the war which in official circles was now considered unavoidable. But it was too late to act: the speakers had resigned their right to speak, and the discussion was over.

The scheme then went through the form of being revised, but the alterations were not a compromise and gave no satisfaction to the minority. The voting took place on the 13th of July. The day before, Darboy had an interview with the Pope, and told

[1] Baunard, *Cardinal Pie*, ii. p. 411.

him the *non placet* votes would be numerous. I daresay, replied Pius, that many will vote *placet juxta modum*, but not more than ten will vote *non placet*.[1] He thought that deference to himself would influence many at the last moment. He was to be undeceived. Of the 692 members still at Rome, 601 appeared to vote. Most of the absent were kept away by sickness. Of the 601, 451 voted *placet*, 88 *non placet*, and 62 *placet juxta modum*. Far the greater number of the *non placets* were French, German, Hungarian, and American. The 13th of July was a memorable day; it was the day on which the famous incident at Ems occurred, the interview of King William and Benedetti which precipitated the war.

It had been hoped to proclaim Infallibility on June 29, the day of St. Peter and Paul. That had proved impossible, and July 18 was now fixed, the anniversary of the day on which the Pope had received the prophecy communicated to the maiden of La Salette. The voting at the public session was to be simply a ceremony, but all the members present would be required to sign an act of submission. The boldest of the opposition decided to attend, to repeat their *non placets*, and refuse to sign. But the most of them were not prepared to incur excommunication. It was decided to make a last appeal to the Pope, and, if this failed, to return home before the 18th. What they asked was that in the section on Infallibility words to the effect *innixus testimonio ecclesiarum* might be inserted. The Pope answered the deputation: There were 88 *non placets*; if you

[1] Nielsen, ii. p. 364; Foulon, *Darboy*, pp. 463 f.; Friedrich, III. ii. 1173-4.

produce 100 for your proposed emendation, I will see what can be done. The Bishop of Mainz threw himself at the Pope's feet, imploring him to save the Church.[1] If Pius was moved, other influences soon rescued him from a momentary hesitation, and on the next day (16th) he sent an intimation that he would as hitherto abstain from interfering with the conclusions of the Council, and confine himself to approving.[2]

Darboy had had no hopes of success, and after the voting of the 13th he circulated a pamphlet which he had written, *La dernière heure du Concile*. A quotation will illustrate its spirit: "All the secular powers have conscientiously respected the freedom of the Council, only one power [the Pope] has in every way restricted it, destroyed it. . . . Let us hope that the excess of the evil will lead to the return of the good. This Council will have only one happy result: that of calling another, assembled in freedom. The Vatican Council will remain barren, in all that has not blossomed under the breath of the Holy Spirit."[3] On the 17th, fifty-six members of the minority sent a joint letter to the Pope, saying that they could not alter their votes, but would stay away.[4]

Five hundred and thirty-five members attended the final session. All voted *placet* except two, Bishop Fitzgerald of Littlerock, in the United States, and

[1] Nielsen, ii. p. 364; Friedrich, III. ii. pp. 1105-7; Pfülf, *Ketteler*, i. p. 111; Foulon, *Darboy*, p. 483.

[2] Friedrich, III. ii. pp. 1182 f., and his *Tagebuch*, p. 390; Quirinus, pp. 803 f.; Ollivier, ii. pp. 341 f.

[3] *Darboy*, p. 6. Cf. Friedrich, III. ii. pp. 1178-80, 1187; Granderath, III. ii. pp. 129-31.

[4] *Collectio Lacensis*, pp. 994 f.

Bishop Riccio of Cajazzo. Cardinal Guidi was one of the minority who sacrificed the intellect and said *placet*. Cardinal Hohenlohe stayed at home.[1] But practically all the opposition, not only the Inopportunists, but those who had contended most strenuously that the doctrine was false, afterwards submitted one by one.[2]

No individual prelate had done more for the definition of the dogma than Archbishop Manning. The Jesuit editors of the *Civiltà Catholica* recognised his services by presenting him with a picture of the great theorist of the ultramontane system, Bellarmine.[3]

We may now examine the text and the bearings of the decree *Pastor Aeternus* which so deeply disturbed the Roman Church, and caused considerable alarm to the governments of Europe.

The first dogmatic constitution on the Church of Christ begins with a short introduction, a part of which I will quote:

In order that the episcopate should be one and undivided, and in order that the whole multitude of believers should be preserved in the unity of communion and faith, by priests united among themselves, the Eternal Shepherd, placing the blessed Peter above the other Apostles, has instituted in him the perpetual principle and the visible foundation of this double unity; that on its strength should be built the eternal temple, and on the firmness of his faith should rise the lofty edifice of the Church,

[1] Only a few of the Cardinal's letters to his brother, Prince Hohenlohe, from Rome during the Council appear to have been preserved, but they form vivid illumination.

[2] Granderath, III. ii. pp. 190-269. Cf. Frommann, pp. 201-11.

[3] Yet cf. Purcell, ii. p. 457.

to be raised as high as heaven. And since the gates of hell are rising on all sides, with a hatred increasing every day against the divine foundation of the Church, to overturn it if it were possible, we judge, with the approbation of the Sacred Council, that it is necessary for the guardianship, safety, and increase of the Catholic flock to promulgate the doctrine on the institution, perpetuity, and nature of the Holy Apostolic Primacy in which the force and solidity of the whole Church consist, and to proscribe and condemn contrary errors which are pernicious to the flock of the Lord.

The constitution consists of four chapters: (1) On the institution of the Apostolic Primacy in the person of the Blessed Peter; (2) on the perpetuity of the Primacy of Peter in the Roman Pontiffs; (3) on the force and character (*vi et ratione*) of the Primacy of the Roman Pontiff; (4) on the infallible *magisterium* of the Roman Pontiff.

(1) The first chapter, in which the scriptural texts which are alleged to support the Primacy of Peter are quoted, ends with the anathema:

If then some one says that the blessed Apostle Peter has not been constituted by Christ our Lord Prince of all the Apostles and visible head of the whole Church militant; or that the same Peter has received only a primacy of honour, and not of true and proper jurisdiction, immediately and directly from our Lord Jesus Christ, let him be anathema.

(2) The second chapter, which lays down the perpetuity, may be condensed as follows:

It is necessary that what Christ instituted in the person of Peter for the perpetual safety and good of the Church should also continually endure in the Church, which founded on a rock will stand firm for ever. All ages know that Peter received the keys of the kingdom from the Redeemer, and that up to the present time and always he lives and presides and judges in his successors, the bishops of the Roman See. Hence every one of the successors of Peter in this Chair possesses, by virtue of Christ's institution, the primacy of Peter and the Universal Church. Thus the "disposition of truth" (*dispositio veritatis* might be translated "economy of truth") abides and Peter has not abandoned the helm. Therefore it was always necessary that all the Church—that is, the faithful in all parts—should look to the Roman Church on account of its primacy, and in it should be members of one body. If then anyone shall say that it is not by Christ's institution or by divine law that Peter has perpetual successors in the primacy over the Universal Church, or that the Pope is not the successor of Peter in the primacy, let him be anathema.

(3) The third chapter begins by renewing the definition of the Council of Florence which attributed to the Pope the primacy over the whole world (*in universum orbem*), and then proceeds:

Accordingly we teach and declare that the Roman Church, God so disposing, holds the principality of ordinary power over all other Churches, and that this power of jurisdiction of the Pope, which is truly episcopal, is immediate; that the pastors and faithful, of every rite and every rank, both individually and collectively are subject to that power by the duty of hierarchical subordination and of true obedience, not only in things which concern faith and morals, but also in those pertaining to the discipline and government of the Church throughout the world; so that the Church may be united. This is the doctrine of Catholic truth.

But so far is this power of the Pope from injuring the ordinary and immediate power of episcopal jurisdiction by which the bishops rule their flocks as true shepherds, their power is asserted, strengthened and indicated by the supreme and universal shepherd.

From this supreme power of the Pope there results for him the right of communicating freely, in the exercise of his duty, with the shepherds and flocks of the whole Church. Therefore we condemn and censure the opinions of those who say such communication can be legitimately hindered or who make it depend on the secular power, pretending that the constitutions of the Apostolic See are not valid, unless confirmed by a placet of the secular power.

As the Pope presides over the Universal Church we teach and declare that he is supreme judge of the faithful and that recourse can be had to his judgment in all causes that come under ecclesiastical competence; that his judgment, than which no authority is greater, can be revised by no one and judged by no one. Therefore those depart from the way of truth who affirm that it is lawful to appeal from his judgments to an Ecumenical Council as to an authority superior to his.

Then follows the anathema of those who deny any parts of this doctrine.

(4) The *fourth chapter* is the most important, for it defines Infallibility, which is called in the title the

infallibile magisterium of the Pope. I must take leave to translate it almost in full:

This Holy See has always held, the perpetual practice of the Church proves, and the Ecumenical Councils themselves, especially those in which the East and the West met in union of faith and charity, have declared that the supreme power of the magisterium is included in the Apostolic Primacy which the Roman Pontiff as successor of Peter holds over the whole Church. Thus the fathers of the Fourth Council of Constantinople, walking in the steps of their predecessors, uttered this solemn profession: "Salvation is first of all to guard the rule of Faith. The words of Christ, 'You are Peter and on this stone I will build my Church', cannot be overlooked; and have been confirmed by facts, because religion has always been preserved immaculate and the holy doctrine always taught in the Apostolic See. So not desiring to separate ourselves in anything from its faith and doctrine, we trust that we may deserve to be in the one communion which the Apostolic preaches, wherein is the entire and true solidity of Christian religion."

Then come quotations from the second Council of Lyons and from the Council of Florence, which I will omit. The text then goes on:

To fulfil this pastoral office our predecessors have always worked untiringly that the salutary doctrine of Christ should be promulgated among all peoples of the earth, and have watched with equal diligence that it should be preserved pure and untainted wherever it was received. Therefore the bishops of all the world, now individually, now in synods, following the long custom of the Churches and the form of the ancient rule, have always referred to this See such dangers as emerged in matters of faith, in order that the harm done to faith might be remedied in that place where faith can suffer no loss or failure. And the Roman pontiffs, according as the condition of time or circumstance dictated, sometimes convoking Ecumenical Councils, sometimes by asking opinions throughout the Church scattered through the world, sometimes by special synods, sometimes by other means furnished by divine providence, have defined that those beliefs should be held which they knew to be in agreement with Holy Scripture and Apostolic traditions. For the Holy Spirit has not been promised to the successors of Peter in order that through its revelation they should publish new doctrine, but in order that with its assistance they should religiously guard and faithfully expound the revelations transmitted by the Apostles, that is to say, the deposit of faith (*fidei depositum*). All the venerable Fathers have embraced, and all the holy doctors have venerated and followed *their* apostolic doctrine, fully knowing that this see of St. Peter remains always untainted by any error according to the Saviour's divine promise made by the Prince of the Apostles—"I have prayed for you, that your faith may not fail, and do you one day confirm your brothers".

This gift then of truth and of faith which does not fail was divinely bestowed on Peter and his successors in this chair that they might perform their high duty for the salvation of all, that they might keep the flock of Christ from the poisonous food of error and nourish it on heavenly doctrine, that the whole Church might be preserved in unity without cause for schism, and on its firm foundation stand against the gates of Hell.

But since in this age, in which the efficacy of the Apostolic office is more than ever needed, there are not a few who object to its authority; we think it necessary solemnly to assert the prerogative which the Son of God has deigned to unite with the supreme pastoral office.

Accordingly we, faithfully adhering to the tradition which goes back to the origin of Christianity, for the glory of the Saviour, for the exaltation of the Catholic religion and the salvation of Christian peoples, we with the approval of the Sacred Council teach and define that it is a dogma divinely revealed, that when the Roman Pontiff speaks *ex cathedra*, that is, when discharging the office of the Shepherd and Doctor of all Christians, in virtue of his supreme apostolic authority defines a doctrine to be held by the Universal Church concerning faith or morals, he enjoys (by divine assistance promised to him in the blessed Peter) that infallibility by which the Divine Redeemer wished his Church to be instructed in the definition of doctrine concerning faith or morals; and therefore such definitions of the Roman Pontiff are irreformable of themselves, and not by virtue of the consent of the Church.

Whoever shall presume to contradict this our definition—which God forfend—let him be anathema.

I have thought it well to quote the whole of this Fourth Chapter of the Constitution, for this reason. Dr. Schulte, Professor of Canon Law at Prague, published a very severe criticism of the dogma immediately after the Council.[1] A reply to it was

[1] *Das Unfehlbarkeits-decret v. 18 Juli 1870.* Schulte employs official documents, though he leans weightily on Acton and—much less—on Kenrick. Cf. his important *Die Stellung der Konzilien, Päpste u. Bischöfe von historischen u. kanonistischen Standpunkte,* to which Fessler directs his attention. Schulte's *Stellung der Konzilien,* pp. 71 ff., 245 ff., deals with fundamentals. Cf. Granderath, III. ii. pp. 309-16.

written by Mgr. Fessler,[1] who had acted as Secretary of the Council; and one of Fessler's points was that Schulte was unfair because he extracted the final definition from the context of the chapter in which it occurs. Fessler contended that the definition assumes a different aspect when taken in connexion with the whole context. The definition must be associated with the historical explanations which precede.

In examining the scope and compass of the dogmatic definition of Infallibility, as to which many have very vague and exaggerated ideas, we must consider in the first place the position of Fessler. He was Secretary of the Council, and his book was approved by the Pope. Its tendency and object are to mitigate and narrow the bearings and consequences of Infallibility so far as he can; at all events, his exposition does not fall into the error of exaggerating the compass of the Pope's *infallibile magisterium*. But it has no official authority. The Pope's approbation did not in any way commit him to Fessler's interpretation. You remember how the two opposite interpretations of the *Syllabus*, that of Schrader and that of the Bishop of Orleans, both received Papal approval.

You observe that in the definition the Infallibility of the Pope is limited in two ways: (1) He is only infallible when he speaks *ex cathedra*; and (2) he is only infallible in matters of *fides* and *mores*.

The term *ex cathedra* is technical, and the defini-

[1] *Das vatikanische Konzilium*, Vienna, 1871, is good, but "The True and False Infallibility of the Popes" is Fessler's real reply to Schulte.

tion explains what it means. The Pope speaks *ex cathedra* when he speaks as *omnium Christianorum pastor et doctor*. But the Church recognises in the Pope other functions besides those of the supreme doctor and teacher of revealed truth. She recognises in him the supreme priest, the supreme legislator in ecclesiastical affairs, and the supreme judge *in causis ecclesiasticis*. Thus, according to the definition, the Pope is not infallible when he is performing the duties of supreme priest, supreme lawgiver, or supreme judge, but only when he exercises the office of the sovran doctor.

Again, there are four principal kinds of ecclesiastical matters which are subject to the sovran power of the Pope: matters of faith, matters of morals, matters of discipline, and matters of ecclesiastical administration. It is the duty of all to obey the Pope in all these things; but the definition declares his infallibility in the first two. He is infallible in matters of faith and morals, but not in matters of discipline and administration. The reason is evident; faith and morals are regarded as permanent and unalterable, discipline and administration as temporary and changeable.[1]

Now how are we to know that an utterance of the Pope on a matter of faith or morals is *ex cathedra*? Are all Papal Bulls, Encyclicals, etc., on such matters to be taken as *ex cathedra*, and if not, by what mark are we to know that such a document contains an infallible decision made *per assistentiam divinam*?

[1] There is a careful discussion in Frommann, *Geschichte u. Kritik des vatikanischen Concils*, from p. 304 onwards. He also gives many relevant references.

Fessler lays down that the decision need not be *ex cathedra* unless the Pope expressly declares his intention of proclaiming a doctrine of faith or morals by virtue of his supreme doctoral authority—as an integral part of revealed truth and one which ought to be held by the Church.

It is clear that the Pope alone can determine the extent, the limits, and the object of a decision *ex cathedra*. In other words, no human authority can dictate to him on the subject. But Fessler rightly points out that this does not mean that the Pope can extend his infallible decisions to judicial matters which are not contained in divine revelation. The Swiss bishops, in a Pastoral Instruction which was approved by Pius IX., explained the matter as follows: "It does not depend on the Pope's caprice or good pleasure to make any doctrine the subject of a dogmatic definition; he is limited to divine revelation and its truth; he is bound and limited by the symbols of faith already existing and by previous definitions of the Church. He is bound by the constitution of the Church; by the divinely revealed doctrine which affirms that beside religious society exists a civil society, and beside the ecclesiastical hierarchy exists the power of temporal authorities invested in their own domain with full sovranty."

Of course a great deal depends in this argument on what divine revelation means. Pope Pius IX. defined the Immaculate Conception of the Virgin, and the Catholic Church, which holds that doctrine, is bound to hold that it is divinely revealed. What is to hinder the discovery being made that the Virgin's mother was also immaculately conceived, and that this is divinely revealed? Revelation is too wide and elastic a conception to constitute a very definite limit or guarantee.

To return to Fessler's doctrine as to the marks by which a definition *ex cathedra* may be known. He applies it to a number of cases. He takes the principal Papal Bulls which have caused most offence by their doctrine of the right of the Pope to control, or interfere with, secular authority, and he professes to show that these Bulls, so far as they lay down this doctrine, do not come within the scope of the Vatican definition, and are not utterances of the Pope speaking infallibly *per assistentiam divinam.*[1]

To examine the validity of Fessler's principles let us take what is admittedly the most drastic of the Papal Bulls in asserting the superiority of Papal to secular authority in the secular sphere, the Bull *Unam Sanctam* of Boniface VIII.[2] It is not only the most drastic, but to an ordinary intelligence it seems unequivocally clear in its meaning. The *Unam Sanctam* lays down the following principles: In the power of the Roman Church there are two swords, the temporal and the spiritual. While both are in the power (*in potestate*) of the Church, the spiritual is to be wielded *by* the Church, the temporal *for* the Church; the former by the hand of the priest, the latter by the hands of kings and soldiers, but by the direction and sufferance of the priest (*ad nutum et patientiam sacerdotis = Papae*). But the one sword must be under the other, and the temporal authority must be subject to the spiritual. The spiritual

[1] Does Fessler suggest that the Pope is sometimes infallible, but nobody knows *when*?

[2] Published in 1302.

power has to institute the secular power and to judge it, if it is not good. Therefore, if the secular power strays from the right way it will be judged by the spiritual power, whence if the highest spiritual power deviates from the right way it will be judged by God alone. Whoever resists this power resists the ordinance of God. The Bull ends with the words: *Porro subesse Romano pontifici omni creaturae humanae declaramus, dicimus, deffinimus, et pronunciamus, omnino esse de necessitate salutis.* "So we declare, say, define, and pronounce that it is entirely necessary for salvation for every human creature to be subject to the Roman pontiff."

The doctrine of the two swords seems to have been first put forward in that form in the twelfth century by St. Bernard. The Bull lays down, as you can see quite clearly, and it supports its several assertions by quotations from Scripture, the doctrine of the *potestas directa* of the Church over temporal affairs. This was the doctrine maintained by the Papacy and ecclesiastical exponents of the Church system from the twelfth to the end of the sixteenth century. It was held by Becket and John of Salisbury as well as St. Bernard. It was triumphantly put in practice by Innocent III. It implied that the secular power was entrusted to princes simply as servants of the Church, who were responsible to the Pope for its exercise. It implied the power of the Pope to depose kings.

In the seventeenth century this doctrine made way for that of the *potestas indirecta*. This new teaching was due to Bellarmine, and was adopted by his order, the Jesuits. It ascribed to the Pope only an indirect power over temporal things. By this the

Pope can only intervene *ratione peccati*, that is, he can only call the secular power to account, command it, or punish it, in case it opposes the higher aims of the spiritual power or endangers religion and the Church. The Pope cannot directly depose a sovran, but he can indirectly contribute to his deposition by declaring in the interests of religion that his subjects are no longer bound to obey him. This indirect power is not secular, it is spiritual, and it only touches the secular sphere if secular authority interferes with religion and so ceases to be secular.

At first this modification of the older theory was so offensive to Rome that Bellarmine's book *De summo pontifice* (1581–3) was put on the Index (by Sixtus V.). But the Popes soon convinced themselves that the new theory virtually amounted to the same thing as the old, and that "indirect power" was a more suitable and convenient expression, and in the seventeenth century Bellarmine's form of the doctrine was established. Whether the power be called direct or indirect, there is no practical difference; the only way, *e.g.*, in which a Pope can depose a prince is by announcing to his people that they are released from their obligations as subjects.

Has this doctrine been reasserted by the Vatican decree? Fessler says no. No part, he contends, of the Bull *Unam Sanctam* is a definition *ex cathedra de fide et monitu*, except the last sentence (which I quoted in Latin), and that refers exclusively to the spiritual power of the Pope, not to the temporal sword.

Now I may first point out that in this Fessler, and others who take the same line (like Martin[1] and

[1] He issued three pastoral letters in 1871.

Hergenröther),[1] differs entirely from the view and interpretation of the Jesuits and ultramontanes who were responsible for the Vatican decree. Here is what the *Civiltà Catholica* said on the subject (and I have explained before what the authority of this organ is) shortly before the Council: "After the Council, the Bull *Unam Sanctam* will acquire its full force. The subordination of the State to the Church is not merely proved by reason; it is the common doctrine of the Fathers and teachers of the Church. Pope Boniface VIII. in his dogmatic Bull *Unam Sanctam* teaches expressly that the secular power must be subject to the spiritual." I might quote other interpreters, such as Molitor, who wrote after the Council, on this subject.

But if we turn to the Bull itself we can see that Fessler's attempt to weaken its authority will not bear examination. He maintains that the purpose of the Bull is simply to define the spiritual supremacy of the Pope. This makes the decree of Boniface superfluous, in fact an absurd anachronism. Nobody denied the supremacy of the Pope in spiritual matters; why in the world should he write a Bull to define it? The occasion of the Bull was the struggle of Boniface with Philip the Fair. Why should the Pope summon a Council to Rome in order dogmatically to define his primacy, which no one disputed? And what is the connexion of the rest of the document with the final definition? The last sentence is introduced by *porro*, a word which Fessler, Hergenröther, and the rest leave out of account. It is regularly used in Papal

[1] He wrote in the *Archiv für kath. Kirchenrecht,* vol. xxv. pp. cxvii-cxxxi.

documents as an alternative phrase to *proinde* or *etiam*. Thus it adds a further and final statement to the preceding declarations, and thus it is quite inadmissible either to refer it merely to the primacy or to discriminate it from the preceding declarations, as though they were undogmatic and it alone dogmatic.

Conscious of the difficulty of thus isolating the final sentence from the whole context of the document, and seeing that Boniface clearly intended to define dogmatically the doctrine of the two swords, Martin curiously holds that though this is true we must consider not the Pope's intention but the actual phrase. And as the phraseology of the last sentence is ambiguous and might, apart from the context, be interpreted of the spiritual power only, we are not obliged to believe that the Pope does possess the power of the two swords. This method of interpretation would reduce the doctrine of Infallibility *ad absurdum*. What sort of infallibility does a Pope possess who intends to define one thing and defines something else? These explanations, I may observe in general, controvert all the common-sense rules of the Roman Canonists, who lay down explicitly that *verba intelligenda non secundum quod sonant sed secundum mentem profantis*.

The true conclusion undoubtedly is that the *Unam Sanctam* of Boniface VIII. has been confirmed by the Vatican decree, and that its doctrine is binding *de fide* on members of the Church of Rome.

The next lecture will be concerned with the fall of the temporal power.

VII

THE FALL OF THE TEMPORAL POWER

Of all countries there was perhaps none to which the proclamation of Infallibility was more obnoxious than Austro-Hungary. Under the Concordat the tendency had been to deprive the laity of the share in the administration of Church property which they had before enjoyed, to transfer the rights of the priests to the bishops and of the bishops to the Pope. But recently, since the Liberal party had come into power, there had been an energetic movement to reverse all this, to associate the laity in religious concerns. The Hungarian bishops had agreed, and a new Church constitution had been adopted for Hungary in October 1869, of which the aim was to free the people from clerical control and relieve the Church from encroachments on the part of the State. The bishops and the government had worked together, and their work was threatened with destruction by the new decrees. On July 30 Beust instructed the Austrian ambassador at Rome to denounce the Concordat.[1] The ground was that the party with which Austria had treated in 1855 had changed

[1] *Collectio Lacensis*, pp. 1716-21. Beust's despatch is in the *Collectio*, pp. 1721-3.

its legal identity by the proclamation of Infallibility.[1]

It is highly significant that the Catholic power, whose supremacy in Germany it had been one of the great objects of the ultramontanes to maintain, and whose loss of that supremacy had been a severe blow to the Vatican, should now declare itself so promptly and so definitely in an anti-Vatican sense.

War was declared on July 19, 1870. If, as most people thought, a French victory was certain, Rome had everything to gain.[2] The strengthening of the French Empire, whose support, though sometimes vacillating, had up to the present secured her temporal power, and recently had rendered the holding of the Council practicable, was not the only consideration; there was also the fact that the defeat of Prussia would prevent the unity, for which Prussia was working, of South Germany with North. But deeply interested though the Vatican was in the war, it is another thing to say that the war was the result of a conspiracy in which the ultramontanes participated. This was commonly believed; and Bismarck asserted it in a speech in the Reichstag in 1874 (December 5): "That when the war was begun against us there was understanding with Roman policy; that the Council was on that account cut short; that the execution of the Conciliar decrees, perhaps even their completion, would have had a

[1] Friedenberg, *Aktenstücke*, p. 155; Wolfsgruber, *Kardinal Rauscher*, pp. 209 ff.; Beust, *Aus drei Viertel-Jahrhunderte*, ii. p. 406; Frommann, pp. 215-25.

[2] Castagnola in the *Rivista storica del risorgimento Italiano*, i. p. 1.

different issue if the French had conquered; that at that time, in Rome as well as elsewhere, the victory of the French was counted on as a certainty,[1] that at the French Court Catholic influences really determined the decision for war, a decision which was very hard for the Emperor Napoleon to take; that peace had been firmly resolved, and this resolve was overthrown by influences whose connexion with Jesuit principles has been proved—of all this I am fully in a position to testify. You can believe me that I know all about this, not only from papers which have been discovered, but also from communications I have received from the circles in question."[2] These assertions of Bismarck must be discounted, because they were uttered at the time of the struggle of the Prussian government with the Vatican and the ultramontanes over the May laws. There is no proof hitherto produced of anything that can be called a conspiracy, but it remains true that ultramontane interests, as well as the interests of Napoleon's government, would have profited by a French victory.[3] The part which the Empress played must be considered uncertain. It is generally supposed that she threw all her influence into the scale for war; and she is commonly reported to have said: "C'est ma guerre!" But now—I have this on private information—she repudiates this responsibility; she denies having even uttered those famous words; and says she can prove by documentary evidence that

[1] Cf. Nurnberger, *Papauté et États de l'Église*, iii. p. 510.

[2] *Politische Reden*, vi. (1893) p. 232; *Gesamm. Werken*, xi. (1929) p. 382.

[3] Busch, *Our Chancellor*, ii. p. 60.

she made attempts to prevent the war.[1] I will only observe that those whose interest it was to consolidate the French Empire might have been waiting for a war, to be declared in 1874, and might have tried to hinder it from breaking out in 1870. This was the true point of the situation. Napoleon wanted war after his alliances were completed, Bismarck wanted it before, and Bismarck forced the hands of the French government.

When the crisis was acute, just before the decisive incident of the Ems telegram, Napoleon sounded Italy and received assurances that this country would not be on the side of the enemy.[2] When war was declared on the 19th, Austria and Italy formed an alliance for an armed neutrality, and the treaty included an article that Austria should ask France to withdraw her troops from the Roman State, the evacuation to take place on conditions conformable to the wishes of Italy. But on July 26 the French Premier, the Duc de Gramont, told the Italian ambassador Nigra that France would not depart from the September Convention, and at

[1] Sir C. Grant Robertson and the Rev. F. A. Simpson do not unhesitatingly accept her proof. Bury had probably just heard of the interview with Maurice Paléologue in April 1906. The Empress was technically correct in denying that she had actually boasted of her responsibility for the war; in any case a circumstantial and authoritative denial of the particular boast of "C'est ma guerre" had been issued as early as 1874. But it does not follow that in *fact* she did not throw all her influence into the scale for war. Denials of that no serious student of the subject would take seriously; and to do the Empress justice she did not always deny that herself. She tells her story in Paléologue's *Conversations with the Empress Eugénie*, published last year. The great work of Oncken on *Napoleon's Rheinpolitik* reveals her important political rôle.

[2] *Nuova Antologia*, Ninth Series, vol. lvi. pp. 9, 14.

the same time sent to Vienna forbidding Austria to interfere with the Roman question.[1] Napoleon confirmed this a week later; and the Empress is reported to have said: "Rather the Prussians in Paris than the Italians in Rome".[2] Yet at the same time Napoleon was preparing to recall the troops. On July 30 Gramont telegraphed to Banneville to prepare the Pope.[3] When Pius learned from Antonelli the French decision, he said: "Now is the time for prayer, but everything will end well".[4] France could explain the recall, as she could explain the retention of the troops, on the ground of the September Convention, and she was now concerned above all things to obtain the help of Victor Emmanuel and 60,000 Italian troops.[5] The King was personally very anxious to help; his daughter, for one thing, was the wife of Prince Napoleon. But Italian feeling was entirely against it, the Lanza ministry was against it, and a council of war, which was held to consider it, proved that it was impossible. It would have meant raising much more than 60,000 to take the field with the French; the frontier on the Bavarian side and the Roman frontier would have to be guarded. There were also republican enterprises to be considered; Mazzini was in Italy; he was presently arrested.[6]

On August 19 the French regiment left Cività Vecchia; their departure was the signal for the cry

[1] *Revue des deux Mondes,* Third Période, 26th part (1878), p. 492.
[2] Cf. Lanza's speech in *La liberazione di Roma,* p. 51.
[3] Favre, *Rome et la République française,* pp. 32 ff., 36 ff.
[4] H. d'Ideville, *Les Piémontais à Rome,* p. 151.
[5] *Nuova Antologia,* Ninth Series, vol. lvi. p. 19.
[6] Tavallini, *La vita . . . di G. Lanza,* ii. p. 5.

for Rome. The government was besieged with clamorous crowds; for the moment it simply placed 30,000 men on the Papal frontiers. Prince Napoleon arrived at Florence on the 20th, but he was to learn that in the face of Italian feeling, Victor Emmanuel, if he sent a single soldier to the help of the Emperor, would be sacrificing his throne.[1]

The ministry were inclined to be dilatory; probably they wished their hands to be forced, and besides this there was friction between the King and the Prime Minister.[2] But the pressure of Rattazzi and the opposition urged them on. A ministerial council was held on August 28 to consider the Roman question—especially, should Rome be the capital of Italy, or what should be its position, and what arrangements should be made for the Papacy. The only definite result of this council was the decision that it should be forbidden to publish the dogma of Infallibility in Italy, though, if it were published, no punishment should be inflicted except in cases where disturbance was caused.

Then came the news of the catastrophe of Sedan on September 2; France was now completely eliminated from the situation; the opposition called on the ministry to occupy Rome immediately.[3] There were strong reasons for haste; there was serious republican agitation, which threatened the Pope as well as the King; and it could hardly be said that the September Convention, which Napoleon had broken

[1] Rattazzi, *Rattazzi et son temps*, ii. p. 340.

[2] Tavallini, ii. p. 28; Castagnola, p. 21; Rattazzi, ii. pp. 348 ff.

[3] Van Duerm, *Vicissitudes politiques du pouvoir temporal des papes*, p. 403.

himself, was binding. This was forcibly represented to the King by the Liberal noble, the Count di San Martino, and under the King's influence the ministry decided to occupy the Papal State,[1] but San Martino was first to proceed to Rome and communicate the decision to the Pope, guaranteeing complete liberty for his spiritual authority.[2] The journal *L'Opinione*, the *journal officiel*, immediately denied the truth of the statement.[3] The reason for this false denial was that the ministry wished to seem to be forced by public opinion to adopt the course on which they had resolved. A manifesto which the Roman republicans issued, when the news arrived that a Republic had been proclaimed at Paris, showed that there was no time to lose. On September 7, the Foreign Minister, Visconti Venosta, issued a circular to the Catholic powers explaining the necessity of the step which Italy was about to take, as one in the interests of the Papacy itself.[4] The action of the Italian government was indeed at the moment somewhat embarrassed by the friction between the King and his Prime Minister, Lanza. There was a double friction, for Lanza opposed the King both on the question of helping France and on the question of immediately occupying Rome. The friction was so great that Lanza resigned, but it was no time for a change of government, and a reconciliation was effected.

San Martino proceeded to Rome to announce the decision of Italy. He saw Antonelli on the 9th, and

[1] Rattazzi, ii. p. 349 ff.
[2] Castagnola, p. 34.
[3] Rattazzi, ii. p. 377.
[4] Printed in Favre, p. 368.

communicated the instruction. The important passage was:

We reserve to ourselves the right to send our troops into Roman territory when circumstances convince us of the necessity, but we will permit the population to arrange for the administration of its own affairs. The government of the King and his forces will confine themselves entirely to conservative action, and to the protection of the imprescriptible rights of the Romans and of the interest felt by the whole Catholic world in the independence of the Pope.[1]

Next day Martino delivered a letter of the King to the Pope in an interview which was somewhat stormy.[2] These communications were met by a simple *non possumus*, and Martino telegraphed to Florence Antonelli's answer that the Pope would not open the gates to Victor Emmanuel's soldiers.

General Cadorna immediately crossed the Roman frontier, and on September 11 issued a proclamation, assuring the people that the Italians had come to protect the liberty of the citizens and that the independence of the Pope would be better guarded by free citizens than by foreign soldiers. Cadorna himself advanced on Rome.[3] A part of the army under Bixio marched to Cività Vecchia, which received him peacefully on September 16. Meanwhile the French government had recalled the French volunteers, who were known as the Antibes legion.

The commander of the Papal troops was General Kanzler, and on the 15th Cadorna sent a formal

[1] Castagnola, p. 38; D'Ideville, p. 169.

[2] Castagnola, p. 39; Rattazzi, ii. p. 356.

[3] The proclamation is in *La liberazione di Roma*, p. 128.

message to him, asking permission to enter Rome for the purpose of preserving order. Kanzler replied that the Pope was determined to resist, and the resolution was not altered by the surrender of Cività Vecchia. On the 17th Cadorna encamped outside Rome.

Count Arnim now intervened. He obtained an armistice for twenty-four hours, hoping to bring the Papal court to reason, but he was not listened to. Cadorna began to attack on the 20th. He had been instructed to seize Rome but not to occupy the Leonine city in which the Pope resided. Pius, of course, was aware that resistance was futile, but he had determined to surrender only at the sword's point, under the sheer pressure of actual violence; and he gave orders to protract the defence till a breach was made in the walls, and then to surrender.[1] The breach was made about ten o'clock near the Ponta Pia; and the foreign diplomatists, who had been with the Pope at his wish all the morning since the attack began, proceeded to General Kanzler, to be present at the arrangement of the capitulation. The terms were that all Rome should be occupied by the Italians except the Leonine city.[2] Next day the Papal army was disbanded and left Rome.

During the next few days, however, it was found necessary to send Italian troops into the Leonine quarter and the Castle of St. Angelo, in order to secure the Pope's safety, in consequence of tumults. This was done by the Pope's own wish.

There were no small apprehensions that the Pope

[1] D'Ideville, pp. 185, 190, 192. [2] Cadorna, p. 203.

might decide to flee from Rome, as he had done himself at the beginning of his Pontificate.[1] Antonelli was strongly opposed to the idea of flight; the General of the Jesuits as strongly advocated it. He thought it would be only for a brief period, that flight would ensure European intervention, that he would come back in triumph and regain his territory.[2] Antonelli knew better than to cherish such a vision. His influence prevailed.

The next step was to incorporate Rome and Roman territory in the kingdom of Italy by a plebiscite. The voting was held on October 2. In Rome itself 40,785 voted for incorporation against a minority of only 46. The total vote in Rome and the provinces together was 133,681 for and 1507 against. The Roman aristocrats voted largely for union, *e.g.* Duke of Sermoneta, the Dorias, the Odescalchis.[3]

After the plebiscite had been presented to the King at Florence, he accepted and confirmed it by a royal decree, in which he promised to secure the Pope by laws of guarantee.[4] Such a promise did not in any way mollify the Pope. His first reply was the Bull *Postquam Dei munere* on October 20, by which he suspended to a more opportune time the reassembling of the Council, because the "sacrilegious invasion" would deprive it of peace and freedom.[5] On November 1 he issued the Encyclical *Respicientes ea omnia*, which placed under the Church's ban

[1] *Politia segreta Italiana*, p. 414. [2] Cappelletti, iii. p. 253.

[3] D'Ideville, pp. 240 ff.; *Allgemeine Zeitung* (Augsburg), October 25, 1870.

[4] Cadorna, p. 279. [5] *Collectio Lacensis*, p. 497.

the usurpers and their coadjutors; Victor Emmanuel was not specified by name.

The advisability of leaving Rome was now pressed more and more on Pius by the Jesuits. The Italian government did their best to prevent the adoption of such a course; they knew that the Pope's flight, though it might not lead to active intervention, would greatly embarrass the government and seem to put them in the wrong. Decrees were issued, by which the Pope's person was declared inviolable as the King's; the Italian press laws were not to apply to the Papal press, and the Papal Bulls and rescripts were exempted from censorship.[1]

But any sort of a reconciliation or *modus vivendi* was extremely difficult, for causes of friction of various kinds were constantly occurring. One of the most serious was the question of a Royal Palace at Rome. The Italians demanded the Quirinal for this purpose. Antonelli refused to give the keys, and the Italian officials broke in the doors.

It is remarkable that the hopes of the Catholics, which had in recent times relied on France, now turned for a moment towards France's conqueror. The Archbishop of Gnesen, Posen, Ledochowski, visited the German camp at Versailles, with an address from his diocese, suggesting that he should intervene on behalf of the Papal States which were the possession of Christendom and could not be touched without violation of the rights of 200,000,000 Catholics.[2] At the same time the Pope proposed himself as a mediator between France and Prussia.

[1] *Allgemeine Zeitung* (Augsburg), November 2 and 6, 1870.

[2] *Ibid.*, November 19, 1870.

The offer was, of course, rejected, and there could be no question of Prussia's interference with Italy.[1] A few days after the Italian occupation of Rome in September, Bismarck had remarked: "The Pope must unquestionably continue to be a sovran, but how? One might do more for him if the ultramontanes were not everywhere opposing us. I am accustomed to pay people back in their own coin."[2]

Victor Emmanuel entered Rome on the last day of 1870. In the following months the main question was to define precisely the relation of the Papacy to Italy. Some governments had thought of proposing a Conference of Catholic Powers; it was an idea which Gladstone and Beust favoured. But it was allowed to drop; it was felt that the discussion would involve great difficulties, and Antonelli recognised that it would probably only issue in an approval by the Powers of what Italy had done. So Italy settled the question for herself by the Guarantee Law of May 13, 1871.

By this law[3] the Pope's person is inviolable under the same sanctions as the King's; but this is not in any way to limit the free discussion of religious subjects, on the ground that such discussion is treasonable to the Pope. The same marks of honour are to be shown by the government to the Pope as to other sovrans, and he is to have the precedence which other Catholic sovrans accord to him. He shall be able to keep the usual number of Papal guards to defend his person and palace. He will receive from the government every year three million and a quarter

[1] Busch, *Graf Bismarck*, i. p. 334. [2] Busch, i. p. 205.
[3] Printed in Scaduto, *Guarentigie pontificie*, pp. 72 ff.

lire, and the same sum will be owed when the Papal chair is vacant. This sum is to enjoy immunity from taxation. The Vatican, the Lateran, with their gardens, and the palace of Castel Gandolfo are to belong to the Pope and not to be taxed. The government guarantees the free assembly of conclaves for election of a Pope; and renounces all right of confiscating papers or any documents in the Papal offices which are engaged in spiritual work. The civil authorities will protect the Papal officials. Foreign ambassadors to the Pope will enjoy the usual immunities of diplomatic agents. The Pope can have his own post office and telegraph, and the right to frank letters and telegrams through the State post offices. He will have perfectly free communication with the Italian bishops and with the whole of Catholic Christendom. These are the most important provisions of the section which deals with the privileges of the Pope.[1] Another section concerns general relations of the State with the Church. Freedom of meeting is guaranteed to the Catholic clergy. Italian bishops are released from the obligation of taking an oath to the King, and the government resigns all claims to assist in the appointments to the higher offices in the Church, while reserving the right of sanctioning episcopal appointments. But it is ordained that only Italian citizens shall be eligible as bishops, except in the case of the six suburbicarian bishoprics which are appointed to Cardinals. All forms of royal permission for publication of ecclesiastical decrees, such as *placet regium* and *exequatur*, are abolished. But ecclesiastical decisions as to

[1] Bolton King, *History of Italian Unity*, ii. pp. 380-81.

Church property shall be subject to government confirmation.

The Bill was not pleasing either to the radicals, who thought that the Papacy was treated too leniently, or to the ultramontanes, who regarded the Parliament which passed it as foes of the Church and the occupation of Rome as a sacrilege. In Italy in general it was regarded as a temporary and opportunist measure. Yet it proved permanent, and in 1878 was included among the fundamental laws of the State. It could, however, at any moment be altered by the Italians themselves, since it is purely Italian law, and no international contract underlies it.

The Pope never recognised the law. He could not compromise, he said, with a violation of right, and his successors[1] have maintained this attitude.[2] He never touched the large annual sum which the law allowed him. Two days after the passing of the law he issued an Encyclical (May 15, 1871) declaring that this law was a *nova et inaudita sacrilegii forma*, and the guarantees were in themselves far from securing the requisite independence to the government of the Church.[3] The word guarantee was an outrage; it implied the imposition of laws upon the Pope, who is appointed the interpreter of divine law and natural law.

In one minor matter the Pope was saved from an injury by the intervention of France. The Italians had intended to confiscate and nationalise the art collections of the Vatican. The French government induced them to forgo this intention.

[1] Till 1929.

[2] *Revue des deux Mondes*, May 1, 1873, p. 118.

[3] Printed in Favre, p. 404.

It was some consolation to Pius that during the last months of 1870 and the year 1871 virtually all the bishops of the minority in the Vatican Council sent him in their complete submission, including the Bishop of Orleans.[1] Hefele, who had assured Döllinger again and again in 1870 that he could and would never submit, nevertheless yielded in April and promulgated the new decrees.[2] His resolution was not strong enough to face isolation. Strossmayer held out; but even he submitted in the next pontificate in February 1881.[3]

Before the occupation of Rome the question had not been settled whether Rome should be the capital of Italy—the residence of the King and the seat of government. The general feeling in Italy was strongly in favour of this change; the general cry was *Roma capitale!* The feeling rested on an idea, on the historic memories which encircled the city of the Seven Hills, on the magic of the Roman name. But many politicians were opposed to the notion; there was an obvious embarrassment in settling the obnoxious sacrilegious government next door to the Papal Palace. The French minister, Jules Favre, was anxious that Rome should be made the titular capital, but that the Parliament and the government offices should remain at Florence.[4] The Lanza ministry hesitated for months; at last in June they decided to yield to the popular wish, and it was settled

[1] Granderath, III. ii. pp. 254-5. Cf. Ollivier, ii. p. 381; Lagrange, *Dupanloup*, iii. p. 165.

[2] Granderath, III. ii. pp. 209-18; Schulte, pp. 217, 220, 223, 227, 230; Friedrich, III. ii. pp. 809-11, 1037.

[3] Granderath, III. ii. pp. 238-40; Schulte, pp. 251, 261, 263; *Collectio Lacensis*, p. 999 c.

[4] Favre, p. 125.

that from July 1 Rome would be the capital of the Italian kingdom. There were other considerations which influenced them in this decision besides the popular pressure. This was the geographical position. Rome even without its historic prestige would have been a compromise between the claims of the North and the claims of the South. The South would have liked Naples—they were dissatisfied with Florence; the North would never have tolerated the selection of Naples.[1] To Rome neither could object. It was also to be taken into account that Rome, if it had not become the capital, would have probably been a hotbed of revolution—ground where republicans of the school of Mazzini would have prosecuted schemes of revolution.

The next important question with which the government had to deal was Church property in Rome and the Roman province. Here more than one-third of the land was in the dead hand. In the interests of economical progress it was of the first importance to apply here the measures which had been applied to Italy in 1867. Accordingly two laws were introduced—one for the dissolution of monasteries, which were quite out of proportion to the number of the inhabitants, and one for the transfer of Church property, by sale and partly by confiscation. In the eyes of the Pope this was an act of robbery;[2] the extreme Radicals thought it too lenient. The Bills were passed in June 1873. On the other hand, a non-government proposal for expelling the Jesuits from Italy was defeated.[3]

[1] Rattazzi, ii. p. 424. [2] Tavallini, ii. p. 97.
[3] Stepischnegg, i. p. 421.

The Jesuits were at this time once more attracting prominent attention in Europe. They were engaged in a bitter struggle in the new German Empire. The antagonism between the Vatican and Berlin had dated from the defeat of Austria, which meant the transference of the supremacy in Germany from a Catholic to a Protestant power. The ultramontanes had made every effort to thwart the political union of Germany under the Prussian king. That union had been accomplished simultaneously with the fall of the temporal power, and for the next year in Italy and Germany alike the mediaeval principles of the Papacy were in sharp collision with the claims of the victorious modern State and the principles of Liberalism. For the Prussian no less than the Italian government found it necessary to rest its policy on Liberalism and Liberal support. The object of the Liberals was to make effective the principle that the State should be omnipotent, and that it should be unsectarian.

The politicians who represented Catholic interests in the new Reichstag organised themselves in the party known as the Centre. Bismarck replied to their opposition by showing favour to the Old Catholics both in the schools and the Church. The Old Catholics were those who refused to accept the decrees of the Vatican Council, and this heresy had caused much ecclesiastical trouble in Bavaria.[1] Döllinger had been duly excommunicated, but the University of Munich replied by electing him Rector by an overwhelming majority of votes.[2] Bismarck

[1] Granderath, III. ii. pp. 343-63.

[2] *Ibid.* pp. 272-90.

forced Old Catholic teachers on Catholic schools. He then abolished the special Catholic department of the Ministry of Public Worship. This was a preliminary to drastic changes. In the first month of 1872 Dr. Falk was appointed Minister of Public Worship, and under his administration was waged the struggle known as the *Kulturkampf*. The name is appropriate and pregnant. It was a struggle between two different ideals of civilisation, between the ecclesiastical order of the Middle Ages and the secular order of modern society.

On the 14th of May Bismarck announced open war in words that are often quoted: "After the dogmas of the Roman Catholic Church which have been recently promulgated, it will not be possible for a secular government to conclude a Concordat with the Papacy, unless that government effaces itself to the last degree and in a way to which the German Empire at least will not consent. Do not be apprehensive. We will *not* go to Canossa, either bodily or spiritually!"[1]

Next day the debate began on a Bill for the banishment of the Jesuits. All the German bishops took the side of the Order, though hitherto they had not loved it overmuch. I will quote part of the speech of Prince Hohenlohe, because it shows the convictions of a temperate statesman who was a Catholic:

If the problem before us were to sit in judgment on the deeds of the Jesuits during the three centuries of their existence, it would indeed be difficult. But this is not the point. We have not to trouble ourselves with the deeds of individual Jesuits, but *with*

[1] Hahn, *Geschichte des "Kulturkampfes" in Preussen*, pp. 72 f.

the Order as a whole. . . . I am heartily ready to concede to a previous speaker that many Jesuits in all times have been distinguished by their learning, blameless lives, and the practice of all works of Christian compassion. . . . But if I concede to individual Jesuits all justice, and if I admit that patriotic Jesuits exist, I must also assert the opinion expressed by Herr von Radowitz, that the advantages to the Catholic Church in Germany which may be expected from the Jesuits stand in no proportion to the disturbances and dangers which their presence entails. . . . The disturbances have appeared, and we are in the presence of dangers sufficiently indicated by the report of the Commission and the petitions against the Jesuits.

What astonishes me about the whole Jesuitical and anti-Jesuitical movements of our day is that the Jesuits and their friends wonder that the modern State abhors them. And yet the Society of Jesus has taken upon itself to make war on the modern State, and its members declare with perfect openness that their purpose is to maintain the unity of ecclesiastical doctrine and the ecclesiastical life in rigid connexion with the Church as the centre of their system. In this of itself lies no danger, but the interpretation which has been put on this original declaration of the Founder contains a distinct declaration of war by the Society of Jesus against the foundations of our life as a State. I will not enter on the question whether the Encyclical of December 8, 1864, and the Syllabus is a decision of the Pope *ex cathedra* or not—this is a question controverted inside the Church itself—but there can be no doubt that this Syllabus forms the guide for the action of the Jesuit Order and the goal of their endeavours. Their writings leave not the slightest doubt about that. . . .

Let me remind you that the Syllabus declares

war on progress, liberty, and modern civilisation; condemns as pernicious errors freedom of the press, freedom of education, religious toleration, and also the freedom of conscience. . . . All writers of the Order advocate these principles; therefore I must accept the fact that the Order adopts them as such; and then the Jesuits marvel when this world condemned by them opens its eyes and asks itself: "Can we tolerate in our midst an institution which is cutting the foundations of our existence from under our feet?" . . .

The Order which advocates these propositions is an organised multitude based on a discipline far stricter than any military organisation. . . . The Order is a power which every member of this meeting has, or at least will have, an opportunity of recognising. Shall we allow this hostile multitude to spread their principles by the power which the cure of souls, the confessional and education give? . . . If we are not to give up our own being, we cannot longer tolerate such a state of affairs. . . .

The conclusion I derive from these premises is that it would be best to agree on a Bill based on the example of Switzerland, which simply forbids the Jesuit Orders.[1]

The Bill against the Jesuits was passed. They and some affiliated congregations, especially the Redemptorists, were banished by an Imperial Statute of the 4th of July from the German Empire. Before the end of the year the German ambassador was recalled from the Vatican.[2]

The government went on to bring the clergy, all of whom sided with the Pope, under the power of

[1] *Memoirs of Prince Hohenlohe*, vol. ii. pp. 74-6.
[2] Hahn, p. 159.

the State. For this purpose they passed three sets of laws, known as the May laws, from 1873 to 1875. Every candidate for the priesthood was required to have studied for three years at a university and passed an examination in history and philology; and to enforce this, bishops were required to give notice of every ecclesiastical nomination. The State claimed the right to supervise theological seminaries. Civil marriage was made obligatory for the whole Empire. In 1875 all monasteries were dissolved. The Pope wrote to the Prussian bishops, declaring the laws null and void.[1] The government demanded a declaration from the bishops that they accepted the new laws, and the salaries of those who refused were not paid. The contest was long protracted; the clergy issuing manifestoes and protests, the government prosecuting and punishing.

It is generally admitted that the *Kulturkampf* was a political mistake. Bismarck virtually went to Canossa afterwards. For a few years later a new strongly protectionist economic policy caused a breach with his supporters, the National Liberals, and he was forced to seek the support of a coalition of the Conservatives and the Catholic Centre. This new policy meant concessions to the Centre, in fact a surrender of the cause for which he had prosecuted the *Kulturkampf*. Practically all the anti-ecclesiastical measures which had been passed were gradually withdrawn between 1880 and 1893, with the exception of Civil Marriage.

Pope Pius IX. died on February 7, 1878, and here I bring these lectures to a close.

[1] Hahn, p. 159.

His Pontificate will always be memorable for two things: for the movement which revived the ecclesiastical claims of the Middle Ages in a most extreme form, and for the fall of the temporal power. The significance of the abolition of the Pope's temporal sovranty, apart from what it meant for the unity, lay in the breach with the mediaeval side. Perhaps we are too close to it still to see fully its great historical importance. Mr. Gladstone was one of the few statesmen who comprehended that it was a change of vast importance—a change which, just because it meant a change in the realm of ideas, might be more profound and far-reaching than the political changes of great magnitude which had recently attracted far more attention.[1] And not less than Prince Hohenlohe did he understand the significance of the *Syllabus* and the Vatican decrees, as he showed in the vehement pamphlet which he published on the subject—*The Vatican Decrees in their Bearing on Civil Allegiance*—in 1874, in which he described the Jesuits as the "deadliest foes that mental and moral liberty have ever known".[2]

We have recently seen a continuation of the struggle in France and another victory for the

[1] Granderath, III. ii. pp. 321-4. Cf. Morley, *Life of Gladstone* (1906 ed.), ii. pp. 123-9, 520; Thureau-Dangin, *Renaissance Catholique en Angleterre*, iii. pp. 159-60; Mourret, *Le Concile du Vatican*, p. 334.

[2] *The Vatican Decrees*, p. 58. Cf. the three articles by Dr. Zirngeibl on "J. v. Döllinger u. die liberale katholische Bewegung" in *Deutschland Ergänzungsblätter*, 1870, October and November, pp. 385, 466, 528. Cf. also Prince Hohenlohe, *Memoirs*, under his diary in November 1870: "When one reflects upon the moral decadence, the complete absence of honour shown by the Bishops, one shudders at the influence which Jesuit control in the Catholic Church exercises upon human nature". In his *Briefe*, p. 106, Döllinger writes: "The Jesuits are incarnate superstition combined with despotism".

modern State. The victory is not surprising. For the fact which gives us most cause for thought, and which I have endeavoured to bring out in these lectures, is that the Papacy, based as it is in mediaeval ideas, has maintained and in many ways increased its moral power and influence, in an atmosphere which is repugnant to it, in the midst of social and political institutions, tendencies, and ideas to which it is fundamentally opposed.

EPILOGUE

EPILOGUE

Professor Bury's final lecture closed with the death of Pius IX in 1878. But a fuller view of "the Papacy in the Nineteenth Century" requires a continuation, at least to 1900. Pius was succeeded by Leo XIII (1878–1903), one of the ablest Christian leaders in all history. It is to him that the Roman Catholic Church owes the almost complete reversal of the conditions which faced it in the 1870's. Bury closed his lectures on an optimistic note: the Church was now gaining ground, despite Pius's revival of an antiquated mediaeval outlook, and also despite the loss of the temporal power. Gladstone's view of the latter (p. 164) was correct; the political change was far more important than the theological, as it involved the total perspective of the papacy, no longer an ecclesiastical (yet earthly) monarchy but a religious and spiritual institution capable of exerting far more influence by its counsels than by its commands. The "prisoner of the Vatican" employed his time and talents without the distraction of political entanglements and obligations.

Leo XIII devoted himself to the strengthening of the Church's internal position, structure, agencies, activities, and welfare. There were fewer broadsides against modern ideas and movements;

instead, there was understanding and sympathy for those caught in the tangled maze of modern movements, social, political, and economic, as well as intellectual. His great encyclical *Rerum Novarum* (1891; Denzinger 3265–71; Bettenson 387–89), dealing with the right to the possession and use of private property, and with laws to safeguard the rights of labor, not only placed the papacy—including Leo's successors—squarely on the side of social justice but at the same time outbade the efforts of Marxists and others to seize the leadership of European labor. (See also his *Quod apostolici muneris,* in 1878; Denzinger 3130–33.) His encouragement of philosophical studies and especially of Thomism (in *Aeterni Patris,* 1879; Denz. 3135–40) marked a new day in modern Catholic theology and theological education: "Inter scholasticos Doctores omnium princeps et magister longe eminet Thomas Aquinas"—this became the motto of a whole new generation of theologians. The influence of this movement spread to other churches and schools of philosophy, and continues to this day. Holy Matrimony and other moral subjects he dealt with repeatedly, e.g. in *Arcanum divinae sapientiae,* in 1880 (Denz. 3142–46), and also the conception of an ideal state, a true "City of God" on earth; see his encyclical *Immortale Dei* of 1885 (Denz. 3165–79). In the *Libertas praestantissimus* (1888; Denz. 3245–55) he dealt with natural law, human law, liberty of conscience and toleration, and recognized the variety in legitimate forms of government—a far cry from the mediaeval conception of "princes." In his *Providentissimus Deus* (1893; Denz. 3280–94) he first grappled with the problems of modern biblical research, insisting upon the Church's duty as teacher of the faith and expounder of Holy Scripture, but facing—for the first time—the questions of variant readings and divergent interpretations. He affirmed the traditional views; but the door had now been opened for further consideration of the problems. In 1902 he appointed the Biblical Commission. The view of the Church set forth in *Satis cognitum* (1896; Denz. 3300–10) of course assumes its supernatural origin and nature, but stresses its mystical reality as the Body of Christ, a view repeatedly quoted and stressed in the speeches at Vatican II.

His rejection of the validity of Anglican Orders, i.e. ordination, in 1896 (in *Apostolicae curae et caritatis*; Denzinger 3315–19; Mirbt 635; Bettenson 385f) was a great disappointment to many, and it has been said that he issued the epistle against his will, under pressure from the Curia. But the view he set forth tallies with his other views, and he may not have required much urging from the Vatican conservatives. The rejection goes a long way back, to 1554, and remains one of the obstacles to reunion at the present day. His theological encyclical on the Holy Spirit (*Divinum illud munus* (1897; Denzinger 3325–31) is a companion tractate to his *Satis cognitum* of the preceding year, and fitly rounds out the selected writings of this great Pope, illustrating both the breadth of his understanding and the depth of his insight. The late Nicholas Murray Butler of Columbia University used to describe him as one of the three greatest public figures of the nineteenth century—the other two (whom Butler also knew) being

Bismarck and Gladstone. Thus his theological eminence and his administrative skill were balancing qualities, and go far to account for the vast change of scene, for the papacy, between 1870 and 1900.

He was known as a humanist, a scholar, even a poet. His Latin style was Ciceronian, and his personality was that of a classical scholar. Cardinal Newman described him as possessing "a depth of thought, a tenderness of heart, a winning simplicity, and a power answering to the name of Leo." In fact, there were qualities of greatness in him which remind us of the heroic Leo I, in the fifth century. But it would be a mistake to describe him as a liberal. He belonged to his own time. His "liberalism" was limited to his social views, which he set forth on the firm basis of moral principles, mainly justice working through love, to be achieved and guaranteed by true charity. Like all the modern popes, he aimed to maintain and continue the standards of his predecessors. Leo firmly adhered to those of Pius IX. He suspected "Americanism" —the proposal to allow lay control of the church's temporalities—for it looked like the ghost of the ancient Lay Investiture which earlier popes had banished! He believed firmly in the temporal power of the popes, and wished to see it restored. There was even talk of a new papal state, the size of Latium (Lazio), ruled by the pope, to be the center of the government of Italy. He went so far as to maintain that Italy would never find peace until the temporal power was restored. And he urged Italian Catholics not to vote or engage in politics until the papacy was relieved of its "painful, precarious, intolerable position." He was a teacher of righteousness, especially of social duty, and he advocated just factory laws, the prohibition of child labor, the establishment of old age pensions, a minimum wage in industry and agriculture, the eight-hour day, with one day in the week for rest, and the revival of the ancient trade guilds. Yet these were only incidental to the total program which he envisioned, *viz.* a Christian state controlled by the church, and headed by the temporal sovereignty of the pope. His reform of the breviary was superficial—the daily offices were still left full of legends—and his devotions to the Blessed Virgin Mary and even the Holy House of Loreto were accompanied by further encouragement for the cult of relics and the granting of indulgences.

The external events of the period which formed the background of Pope Leo's reign were of immense importance, both in their own time and for all that was to follow. Never before had the "roaring loom of time" produced a wider, heavier, more variegated fabric! It seemed to be an era of peace. At long last the nations had agreed to "live and let live." Despite French demands for a "revenge" against Germany and the recovery of the lost provinces of Alsace and Lorraine, the booming business and exchange of goods, the hum of the factories, the rising prosperity of Europe seemed to be a guarantee that the dream of perpetual World Peace was about to be fulfilled. There were protests. When James Henry Breasted was a graduate student at the University of Berlin, early in the nineties, the hungry unemployed laborers gathered outside the gates of the Palace Gardens, crying out for *Brot und Arbeit*—Bread and Jobs! The colonial expansion of Europe in Asia and Africa provided an endless source of raw materials, and occupation for all the superfluous clerks and second sons and white-collar workers in the "old" countries. The American "open door" likewise beckoned: between 1850 and 1900 a total of 16,659,406 immigrants were freely admitted to the United States. This figure was exceeded during the next fifty years, when 20,201,876 arrived. The banner decade was 1901–10, when almost nine million entered.[1] Instead of being a drain upon Europe's population, "colonialism" and migration served to maintain an economic balance. Not only did peace appear to be permanent, but also prosperity. In Great Britain the ratio of wages to prices had risen almost 50 per cent in the fifty years ending with the First World War. Even so, the wealth of those at the top had increased still more, and the promise of earthly happiness to all who shared the new age of Iron and Steam, Manufacture and World Trade, appeared to be insured with infallible guarantees. Democratic reforms were in the air, but awaited the Liberals of 1906–14 for full enactment, when the costs of the reforms were covered by heavier taxes on the well-to-do, the large landowners, and the rich heirs.

A similar course was run in France, which had recovered in a short time from the disastrous war with Germany into which Bismarck had lured the simple-minded Napoleon III. Despite the chronic

[1] See *Encyclopedia Americana,* XIV, 715.

instability of "governments" and cabinets, and the constant turmoil of half-hearted but highly emotional and expensive preparations for *la Revanche* upon the enemy, French prosperity steadily increased. It is said the housewives of France paid the war indemnity; they also provided the sinews of war for the chauvinists' appalling project. And they also—if somewhat more reluctantly—provided the man-power. The bourgeoisie was dominant—and secure; and it was largely anti-clerical. During the decade following 1871 the Church was on the side of the luckless royalists, who still hoped for reinstatement; for the Church identified the Third Republic with the aims and ideals of the French Revolution. But republicanism definitely triumphed in 1879. Even years later, in 1892, Pope Leo urged French Catholics to accept the new situation and cease from the hope and the effort to effect a Bourbon restoration. But his counsels fell on deaf ears. The Boulanger Rebellion of 1887–89 had only increased the strength and prestige of the Republic. The terrible Dreyfus affair (1894), with its explosion of hidden antisemitism, was another device of the monarchists to discredit the Third Republic. But the plot boomeranged, and the army's acquittal of Alfred Dreyfus's accuser brought down the moral standing of the monarchists (many of them Catholics) to the absolute nadir. The result was a fresh tide of anticlericalism that lasted for another decade. In 1905 the Republic repudiated the Concordat of 1801 (Mirbt 558f), turned against the church schools and the religious orders, and disestablished the Catholic Church itself. This struggle formed part of the background of Modernism, which was especially strong in France.

As in Great Britain, so across the Channel the tide of prosperity ran high, and the concomitant expansion and exploitation of foreign interests won back the clerics, in a measure, as new territories in Asia and Africa opened the way for foreign missions, while the fresh flood of prosperity paid for them. Social legislation to benefit the lower classes, to protect women and children, to provide compensation for working-men, and to recognize the trade unions marked France as one of the leading nations in the modern world. Thus loss and gain were balanced, and the nation moved on toward its day of reckoning in 1914.

Meanwhile the German Empire enjoyed a level of prosperity (after 1870) which outstripped all competitors on the Continent, and with its skilful combination of industry and scientific research threatened to leave behind all competitors everywhere. But under the impetus of Bismarck's principles, and faced with the necessity of holding together and uniting into one a vast territory which, until comparatively recently, had been broken up into scores of tiny independent states, the military program of Germany was also greater than that of any other nation. Europe became an "armed camp," and the high seas were covered with flotillas of warships. Likewise in consequence of its devotion to Bismarck's doctrines ("blood and steel" now replacing "blood and iron"), the nation made very little progress toward social reform. Only as late as 1918, at the end of World War I, Max Weber observed that "bourgeoise security is now at an end." And an eminent German philosopher could say, in 1944, that World War II was really the final collapse of feudalism in central Europe.

Bismarck had climaxed his successful war with France, his seizure of Alsace and Lorraine, the union with Bavaria and the incorporation of the southern states in the new empire, by opposing the Catholic Church, especially after its loss of the Papal States on one hand and the Infallibility Decree on the other. The latter he understood—or pretended to understand—to be a device for a renewal of papal control over civil governments, or at least for an assertion of earthly sovereignty and the right to dictate secular policies. The political situation of the Pope was reassuring, from his point of view, but the loss of the temporal power—especially as its recovery was now advocated in Rome—might easily drive the Catholics to overt action against secular states. Moreover, Bismarck stood on the side of modern science against the reactionary doctrines of the *Syllabus* of Pius IX and the superstitions still encouraged by Leo. But his "May laws" in 1873, which formed part of Bismarck's *Kulturkampf* against the Catholic Church, were gradually rescinded between 1880 and 1887. It was Pope Leo's insistence upon their repeal, tempered by his consideration for a man hard to command, that resulted in this slow but sure process. Leo's arbitration of the rival claims of Germany and Spain to the Caroline Islands, in

1885, helped to assure the repeal of the objectionable legislation, which would have made the Church dependent upon the civil government.

From now on, the Center Party was increasingly powerful, and the German government responded more and more favorably to the Church's requests for cooperation and appeals for funds. In fifteen years, from 1883 to 1898, the number of cloisters in Germany increased from 922 to 2873; by 1912 there were over 7000, with more than 70,000 members of religious orders.[2] The tide had definitely turned, and the Iron Chancellor's church policies were at last forgotten—or disguised. Bismarck's military policy, *viz.* the creation of a huge army and (after 1898) navy, was still central, and moved steadily onward toward Armageddon. The vast industrial prosperity of Germany only lent an assurance of success to whatever military or naval undertaking seemed desirable to those in control of Germany's destiny. Alliances were formed abroad to meet and counteract the threat of other groups, bound together by treaties. Trade agreements supported the military commitments, and the military supported the trade. It was a vicious circle: not the "iron ring" of surrounding enemy nations about which Germany pretended to have a just complaint, but the whole reciprocal process of prosperity plus expansion plus increased military strength plus more expansion plus more prosperity, a fatal process which blinded the eyes of those who saw only the prosperity, and the prospects of more. The *Drang nach Osten* which proposed to

[2] Heussi, *Kompendium,* § 116 *g.*

take over the Balkans, South Russia, Turkey, and Mesopotamia, as its first step, and to build a Berlin-to-Bagdad railway, as a step toward further expansion—this gigantic scheme was supported by millions of theorists, economists, industrialists, politicians, and dreamy clerks. World War I was to have resulted in its achievement. But the positive values of the proposed stabilization of the Balkans and the further development of the East were lost and forgotten in the too obvious mania of *Schrecklichkeit* and planned terrorism with which Germany set about achieving the plan.

Fortunately for Leo XIII, the "Peace Pope," he died in 1903, before the catastrophe of World War I began. But it is not at all unlikely that the hope of his later years, to which he ever more frequently referred, *viz.* a society headed once more by the temporal power of the papacy, a just society under God and God's representative, may have been a desperate alternative to impending chaos. Anyone with eyes to see could discern the lengthening shadows as dark night descended, and "the lights went out all over Europe." But how few there were who saw what was coming!

Leo's successor was Pope Pius X, who reigned during the fatal eleven years (from August 4, 1903 to August 20, 1914) which led up directly to the First World War. He was a gentle, saintly man (canonized in 1954), whose avowed aim was *omnia instaurare in Christo,* "to renew all things in Christ" (Ephesians 1.10, Vulgate). And he died while the "guns of August" were destroying half the world, and unleashing demonic forces which have not yet been brought under control by civilization.

He suffered much grief from the misfortunes of the Church in France, from the growing militarism of the time, and from the threat of dissension and even schism within the Church itself. The first two of these causes of grief have been described; the third was the movement known as Modernism. This was an attempt to reform the Church by leading it to accept the results of both modern science and modern historical and biblical criticism—i.e. research or investigation, involving the use of the scholar's judgment (in Greek *crisis,* or criticism). According to its advocates, this was the way that led to a renewal alike of the Church's intellectual freedom and its greater spiritual depth. The beginnings of the movement may be traced to liberal Catholic scholars in Germany during the latter part of the 19th century: Hermann Schele, the theologian, and Johannes Janssen, Heinrich Denifle, Franz Kraus, the church historians. Among them were some who hoped to see the Church set free from its overwhelming inheritance from the Middle Ages and its cultural burden bequeathed by the age of baroque.

But it was in France, and to only a less degree in England, that Modernism got under way after the turn of the century. Alfred Loisy, a professor in the Collège de France, was its leader. His famous book, *L'Évangile et l'Eglise,* "The Gospel and the Church" (1902), which was in form or pretext a reply to Adolf Harnack's *Das Wesen des Christentums,* "The Essence of Christianity" or (as in the English translation) "What is Christianity?" (1900), was widely read and quoted. His thesis, briefly stated, was this: "What Christ announced was the Kingdom of God; what came was the Catholic Church." This was essentially an apologetic argument for Catholicism, based upon the then-popular apocalyptic view of the Gospels and the teaching of Christ, rather than upon Harnack's avowed Ritschlianism (which Loisy combatted), with its confident assumption of solid and substantial modern progress, and with a prominent niche in the sanctuary reserved for Prince Otto von Bismarck.

In France, Loisy's chief follower was a priest, Albert Houtin. In Italy, Romolo Murri, Antonio Fogazzaro (who wrote a popular novel, *The Saint,* also translated into English), and the more scholarly Ernesto Buonaiuti, were leaders in the movement. In England, the chief advocate was Fr George Tyrrell, S.J., whose popular writings, especially his *Christianity at the Cross Roads* (1910), were read literally by "the millions" for whom he wrote, and won a favorable hearing for the Modernist proposals. Many scholars were influenced by the movement, even in the Church of England and among the Nonconformist clergy, though not all acknowledged their allegiance or joined the Modern Churchmen's Union, whose journal was widely read and has continued in publication for many years. The eminent religious philosopher and biblical critic, Baron Friedrich von Hügel, though no Modernist, sympathized with many of their views. It was his article on the Fourth Gospel ("John, Gospel of St") in the eleventh edition of the *Encyclopaedia Britannica* (1911) that induced the veteran biblical scholar William Sanday, the foremost New Testament critic in Great Britain and in the English speaking world, to renounce the Johannine authorship of that work. Von Hügel's *Mystical Element in Religion* (two vols., 1908), his book on *Eternal Life* (1913), and his famous *Essays and Addresses on the Philosophy of Religion* (two vols., 1921–26) made a deep and permanent impression upon two generations of English-speaking scholars and students, and upon many others outside Great Britain and North America.

It looked at first as if even the Curia might be persuaded to approve the Modernist movement—though no one liked the title!—but slowly and steadily the scale tipped against it, and in 1907 Pope Pius issued his "new Syllabus," *Lamentabili sane exitu* (Denzinger 3401–66; Mirbt 652), and the encyclical *Pascendi dominici gregis* (Denz. 3475–3500; Mirbt 653), ordering its abandonment as the quintessence of all heresies.

Like the record of an Old Testament king, the rest of the acts of Pius X, "are they not written in the book" of documents for his reign, chiefly on questions of biblical introduction (concurrently by the Biblical Commission), e.g. on the sources of the Gospels, the text of Mark, the authorship of Hebrews—all decided from the ultra-conservative point of view (see Denzinger 3503–93 *passim*). He also wrote on daily communion (Denz. 3375–83), and finally a decree on the study of St Thomas (Denz. 3601–24), a reply to the philosophic and scientific inquiries of the day.

His unfortunate encyclical in 1910, *Editae saepe* (Mirbt 656), in which he took the occasion of the centenary of the canonization of St Charles Borromeo to strike out against the Protestant Reformers, described them as "enemies of the cross of Christ," who "mind earthly things," "whose god is their belly." "Woe to those who call evil good and good evil," and have unleashed a plague of errors! This encyclical, fortified with tirades borrowed from holy writ, dropped like a thunderbolt among the evangelical leaders of Germany. No excuses could explain the Pope's language, nor were assurances possible that he had been misinformed! It was obvious that His Holiness had taken counsel of his fears, and was still operating on the level of Pius IX, condemning what he could not understand, and unable to grasp the point of view of those who differed with traditional Romanism. The pity is that the energies of a good man should be so sadly misdirected, and that his only preparation for the dark night now descending on the earth was to hide away in a still darker cellar of theological conservatism, where, without danger of immediate contradiction, he could issue his sharp diatribes and thundering anathemas.

He favored "Catholic Action" by laymen, under the guidance of their pastors, in setting up new social and moral standards. Under his leadership the *Corpus Iuris Canonici,* the great collection of Roman Catholic Canon Law, was revised between 1904 and 1914. As Fr Joseph Collins has written of him, "He remained at heart a country pastor," and in his last will and testament he said: "I was born poor, I have lived poor, I wish to die poor." It is said that he died of a broken heart over the war he could do nothing to prevent.

We have already passed beyond the border of the nineteenth century, but in order to see the full development of tendencies already at work a century ago it is necessary to survey, even briefly, the course of events down to the present.

The twenty-five years from 1914 to the outbreak of World War II was an apocalyptic quarter-century, truly a period *zwischen den Zeiten.* The new territorial divisions, designed to insure lasting peace, and a League of Nations intended to give proper representation to minority populations, under the principle of "self-determination," turned out to be as provocative as any previous scheme for balancing (or counter-balancing) European or world stresses. The problems of minorities (thirty million people in all!) without transfer of populations, the assignment of mandates to responsible nations who were to care for their interests, the arrangements for temporary occupation of the coal-rich Saar Basin by France, and the permanent isolation of Danzig as a "free city" remote from the German border—all these proved to be friction points of great and increasing seriousness. With the rise of local parties dedicated to freedom or independence, and especially the rise of Nazism in Germany, the threat of renewed warfare rose steadily. The failure of the United States to join the League of Nations, due to its traditional "isolation" from European quarrels and entanglements, seemed to be justified by the conditions which, alas, the United States itself had helped to aggravate. The positive achievements of the League, e.g. the Permanent Court of International

Justice (the World Court) and the International Labor Organization, were overshadowed by the growing threat to peace. Russia was in the throes of a revolution which began before World War I had ended; its repercussions and wider influences were felt far and wide, especially in Germany, where fear of "Bolshevism" and the determination to prevent its spread caused the downfall of the relatively weak German Republic and the rise of the fanatical National Socialist party, the Nazis under Adolf Hitler. The wars in Spain and Ethiopia were ominous of "more to come." The representatives of the old order were still clinging desperately to their inherited privileges; the protagonists of revolution were equally determined, and increasing in strength. Communism was as real a threat to nations still rooted in ancient and mediaeval autocratic or aristocratic ways as it was to modern capitalist patterns of life.

By 1935 Germany was again preparing to strike on two fronts. The screaming dictator of Italy, Benito Mussolini, was only second in influence to Hitler, whose control of the new generation was likewise achieved by emotion and shouting, the cry against injustice: the Treaty of Versailles which had concluded World War I was blamed by Germany for all of Europe's ills. The other nations were preoccupied with their own affairs, and sat in silence like birds on a low bough, transfixed by the fierce gaze of an advancing snake. Finally, in September 1939 the attack on freedom began. Hitler invaded Poland. This led to declarations of war by France and Great Britain, and Germany's war was again being fought on two fronts, east and west. Before it ended, almost the whole world became involved, and battles were fought on every continent and on many a distant island and upon the waters of all the seven seas. Again, as in World War I, the United States was compelled to share in it. And again, as in the earlier war, a German victory was lost when only a hand's reach away. This time ten million lives were sacrificed to halt the progress of insane national ambition. Countless other lives were lost in the aerial and submarine attacks on civilian populations. Property losses were incalculable, including irreplaceable treasures of art—e.g., the city of Dresden, that ancient center of art and learning, was obliterated from the air. Under Hitler and his savage associates, the antisemitic hatred which had been indigenous in Central Europe since 1870 or thereabouts was fanned into flame, and six million Jews were put to death in concentration camps, in gas ovens, and in torture chambers.

This time, the World War was followed by judicial trials of the culprits who had planned and perpetrated crimes against humanity, and instead of the defunct League of Nations a new organization, the United Nations, was set up, with stronger support than the old League had received, and this time with the United States assuming a central position of responsibility for its success.

In every way the world has changed phenomenally since 1939. The British Empire, for example, despite Winston Churchill's protest against its dismemberment, has become the British Commonwealth of Nations. The atomic bomb, and its vastly swifter delivery both by plane and by intercontinental missile, not to mention by submarine, has enormously increased the threat to peace—but equally the guarantee of peace, under penalty of swift annihilation, whoever launches it. The scientific and social advances of the new age, especially in extra-terrestrial aviation, in medicine and biology, in physics and in psychology, including psychoanalysis, in the spread of social welfare and mass education, and now the war on poverty, the aid to underdeveloped nations, the universal Peace Corps, already operated by several nations, the destruction of slums and the provision of decent housing for all classes of people, the integration of alien and separated groups, the steps taken at long last toward real justice for the Jew, the Negro, and the Indian—these advances mark off our time from all preceding generations, certainly from those in the nineteenth century. And yet the paths which have led to this present progress can be seen emerging from the forest back in the 1870's, '80's, and '90's. This shifting scene, since 1870, with all its catastrophes and recoveries, emergencies and fresh efforts, has been not only the background of the history of the papacy since the First Vatican Council but a real part of that history; and the papacy, in turn, has formed a real and important part of world-history. It is no longer shunted to a siding, off the main line of advance, as it was in 1870 and the years following. The "prisoner of the Vatican" has long been released (by the Lateran Treaty of 1929), and is once more a world figure, with representatives of the Church in many nations, so that his voice "goes out into all lands." The spectacle of the Second Vatican

Council could never have been imagined in the days of its predecessor in 1869–70, nor could the recovered influence of the Roman Catholic Church after the crushing blows it received in the middle of the nineteenth century.

The successor to Pope Pius X was Pope Benedict XV (1914–22), a trained diplomat from the school of Leo XIII. Since the World War involved millions of Catholics on both sides, the papal policy was really neutrality and impartial friendliness to both sides. Himself of noble lineage, and having spent some years as a representative of the Vatican at Madrid, Pope Benedict enjoyed high connections and contacts all over Europe. His wise counsels increased the respect for the papacy on both sides. Whereas there had been only twenty representatives of foreign governments at the Holy See in 1914, when the war ended there were thirty-one. Benedict had pleaded with the rulers on both sides to settle their differences at the conference table, not on the battlefield. He did his best to prevent the spread of the war to involve Italy in conflict with Austria, both "Catholic" countries. But he was unsuccessful. He rebuked the violation of Belgium's neutrality, and in 1917 attempted to mediate between the belligerents (see Mirbt 660f). In spite of the war he promoted the world-wide missions of the Church (see his Apostolic Epistle of November 1919, in Mirbt 664). His interest in theological study is reflected in the encyclical *Ad beatissimi Apostolorum* (1922), in which he insisted that by its nature the Catholic faith is unchanging, and can be neither supplemented nor diminished.

''One must either maintain it as a whole, or reject it as a whole'' (Denzinger 3625). He made it a rule (oft quoted since then!), ''Nihil innovetur nisi quod traditum est'' (No innovation except from tradition!), a sentence borrowed from Pope Stephen in the year 256, in a letter addressed to St Cyprian of Carthage (Denz. 110). More briefly stated, it ran: ''Non nova, sed noviter,'' which means, Not something new in substance but something new in manner of presentation—a sentence which also echoes St Vincent of Lerins, ca. 450. The biblical decisions of his reign reflect this attitude, as does also the revision of the Canon Law, and the whole outlook of Catholic missions, propaganda, and education. Even in church-state relations there was no change of the Canon Law. The reason for this was presumably that any change undertaken thus early might have jeopardized the progress already made toward agreement with the Italian government, destined for fulfilment in 1929 and the years following. In the still disturbed and uncertain state of affairs in all governments everywhere, no new arrangements were possible during Benedict's reign. Only the exchange of visits, and the welcome to the Vatican of distant embassies, like that of the Japanese Crown Prince in 1921, were laying a foundation of friendship and good will which would make possible closer relations for the Church.

Pope Benedict was succeeded by Pope Pius XI (1922–39), a wise choice for leader in an era of reconstruction, as it was hoped it would be. He was a quiet, scholarly man who had been for twenty years a librarian in the Ambrosian Library at

Milan and then Prefect of the Vatican Library in Rome after 1914. He saw service as a diplomatic representative, "apostolic visitor," and then nuncio, in Poland, and his tact and skill were evident in the concluding of the Lateran Treaty with Mussolini in 1929, which ended the almost sixty-year alienation between the papacy and the Italian government. It recognized once more the temporal power of the pope, at least in the limited area of Vatican City, Castel Gandolfo, the pope's summer home, and one or two other small areas, and it made possible free diplomatic exchange with other nations. Religious marriages (in Italy), religious teaching in schools, episcopal nominations and appointments, titles to church property, and compensation for territories seized by the government in 1870, an amount totaling one and three-quarters billion lire, were all included in the treaty.

His famous encyclicals on marriage and family life and the education of children, *Divine illius Magistri* in 1929 (Denzinger 3685–98) and *Casti connubii* in 1930 (Denz. 3700–24), his reaffirmation of Leonine principles in the *Quadragesimo anno* of 1931 (Denz. 3725–44; Bettenson 389–93), his warning against Communism in *Divini Redemptoris* in 1937 (Denz. 3771–74) and his equally strong warning against the abuse of political power in *Firmissimam constantiam* the same year (Denz. 3775), laid a scholarly and carefully reasoned foundation for the present day teaching of the Church in these areas of personal, domestic, and public ethics. His powerful stand in *Mit brennender Sorge* (1937) outspokenly condemned Fascism and the principles of Hitler, who by this time had closed 20,000 Catholic schools in Germany and condemned hundreds of members of religious orders, chiefly teachers, on false charges of immorality. This demonstration of the impossibility of "doing business with Hitler," which was discovered only much later by Americans and many others, should be recalled when his successor's failure to stop Hitler's persecution of the Jews is described and deplored. Relations with France were better, as might have been expected. Jeanne d'Arc had been canonized in 1920 (Mirbt 665), and the Church's provision for the needy during and after the First World War was well known. The Vatican had also sent relief to Germany during and after the blockade, especially food for children. But Hitler, being mad, remembered only what suited his foul purposes. Pius also canonized many saints, including Robert Bellarmine, John Fisher, Thomas More, Bernadette Soubirous of Lourdes, and the Jesuit martyrs in North America. He was also an ardent supporter of the Church's foreign missions.

Pope Pius XII (1939–58) was another descendant of a noble Italian family long devoted to the papal service, but the first Roman to be chosen since 1730. Like several of his recent predecessors, he had been abroad in the diplomatic service of the Vatican, and was known for his wide interests in every area of human culture, welfare, and need. Like Pope Benedict, whose reign began with and included the First World War, that of Pius XII tallied with World War II; like him, he also did everything possible to avert the conflict. He was also tireless in providing for the needy and the suffering. His deep interest in foreign missions is reflected in his encouragement of a native episcopate wherever possible, a policy whose fruits were conspicuous at the Second Vatican Council, with native bishops present from all parts of the world. He also revised the rules for fasting before communion, making it possible for working people, especially night workers, to receive the Sacrament at odd hours when they were free to attend; he simplified some of the rubrics in the Missal and Breviary, and restored the Easter vigil and evening masses. He was a constant student, even in his later years when increasingly ill. I saw him once in the Vatican Garden, walking slowly with an open book in hand—a friend told me it was a Russian grammar, which would enable him to converse in that language when the time came for renewed relations with the Russian Church and people, or when religious emissaries (a Slavic Order) could be sent to Russia. In 1950 he celebrated a Holy Year, when over nine million pilgrims visited St Peter's. It had been hoped that the excavations beneath the basilica would locate and identify the remains of the Apostle Peter, or at least find convincing proof of his interment there, beneath the area of the high altar which is still called the *confessio* (where Peter died confessing his faith). Unfortunately, the evidence was not forthcoming, and the burial there remained only a probability.[2] The same year, as if in compensation, but really

[2] See the recent article by Professor Erich Dinkler, "Petrustradition," in the new edition of *Religion in Geschichte und Gegenwart,* Tübingen 1961, which sums up the evidence; or my book, *Rome and Reunion,* Oxford 1964, chap. 8.

to celebrate the Holy Year, the Pope proclaimed the doctrine of the Assumption of the Blessed Virgin Mary (Bettenson 395f; Denzinger 3900–04). His great encyclical *Mystici Corporis* (1943; Denz. 3800–22) expounded the doctrine of the nature of the Church which had been growing in importance since 1870, and his outstanding *Divino afflante Spiritu* (also 1943; Denz. 3825–31) was hailed as the *magna carta* of biblical studies in Roman Catholicism.

A long play, *The Deputy,* by Rolf Hochhuth, has brought against Pope Pius XII the charge that he failed to use his influence to prevent or stop Hitler's murder of the Jews in Germany, Poland, and elsewhere. In view of the known character of Pius XII, it seems unlikely that he made no effort, and did not speak out. The attitude of the papacy was clear. His predecessor, when Mussolini began the persecution of the Italian Jews, defended them and roundly affirmed, "We Christians are also Jews." Moreover, the Pope's act of sheltering all the Jewish refugees he could accommodate in Vatican City and his provision of care, food, and clothing, for them and their children; the refuge found for them in churches and religious houses in Italy, Germany, and elswhere; his intervention to prevent the destruction or even the desecration of the famous Old Synagogue in Rome (the one beside the Tiber, near the Theatre of Marcellus)—all this makes it improbable that Pius XII can have remained silent. Only the Vatican archives will show whether or not he tried to intervene, and these are not yet available. Whether he should have spoken aloud to the world, in condemnation, is another question. Other heads of ecclesiastical bodies were urged to speak out, and declined, thinking an appeal to Hitler or a protest against his misdeeds would only increase his fury and result in the murder of many more victims, Catholics and perhaps Protestants as well as Jews, and likewise many non-Christians as well. Hochhuth overrates the power of a word from the Pope: this was no longer the eleventh century, and Pius XII was not Gregory VII. It is suggested that Pius was urged to speak out even before the slaughter of the Jews began, and ignored the request.[3] And it is said that he was cold, austere, and academic, and did not react instantly to stories of cruelty and torture—as Pope John would have reacted. It is also said that he hesitated to weaken the only defense of Western Europe against Communism—this dilemma completely neutralized his will to aid the Jews. Still another explanation is that he did not wish to place before the millions of Catholics supporting the German and Italian cause the hard choice between loyalty to their leaders and obedience to conscience—a dilemma which Protestants in theory believe to be unreal, since it is Christian teaching that one must never violate his conscience, and since decision, *Entscheidung,* is the foundation of Christian, not to say human, character: the Protestant is not used to authoritative external guidance and direction, telling him what is right and wrong and what he must pursue and what avoid. His conscience is in no man's keeping but

[3] By Cardinal Tisserant; see *New York Times,* March 27, 1964, p. 2.

his own. But on the contrary, how many Christians —I *mean* to include Protestant Christians—raised any question about other kinds of atrocity, in either World War? Again, it is said that Hitler had definite plans to seize the Pope and put him in a concentration camp, and then perhaps execute him —intending thus to "smash the papacy once for all." It is said that the Vatican staff had their bags packed, ready to be taken to a concentration camp any day.[4] But it is strange that in a church which honors martyrdom its leaders should choose silence and safety when the hour for testimony arose. A friend of mine who was in the landings at Leyte and Okinawa remarked, when he heard this explanation, "Nothing could have done more to break Hitler's power and stop the massacre of the Jews than the martyrdom of the Pope. Why did he hesitate?"

But the case is still *sub judice*. When the papal archives are fully available it may turn out that Pius did more than we suppose. In any event, *Der Stellvertreter* ("The Deputy" is a poor translation) was, in reality, the heroic priest who identified himself with the Jews and died with them, their champion, their representative, their substitute—as did others, heroic priests, teachers, nurses, and nuns. *That* is the subject of the play, I believe, not the Pope's failure to stop Hitler or even to speak out against his diabolical cruelties. If the title means more, it may point to a contrast between the young priest and the Head of the Church.

[4] See Abp. Egidio Vagnozzi in *New York Times*, March 21, 1964.

But even if the Pope failed, supposing he tried, or failed to speak out, for lack of nerve or because of a dilemma, *did any one else try?*

As the present Pope, and also the Vatican Council, affirm, the sin was the sin of us all. And as in the case of the popular charge against the Jews that they "killed Christ," the charge is also diabolical. Jesus was put to death by a cowardly and corrupt Roman procurator. He was crucified as an insurrectionist, a false charge (see Luke 23), though at the instigation of a handful of his enemies, jealous of his growing influence with the people. Like them, we too, in this twentieth century, were "consenting unto his [their] death." For when we heard of it we merely shuddered at the ghastly news and then went on about our daily business. Like the thirty-seven feeble citizens who watched a young woman being murdered, not long ago, and failed even to notify the police, we all failed to *do* anything about the appalling crisis. Only at long last, after Pearl Harbor, did we Americans awake to the fiendish horrors of Hitler's war against the defenseless, including his murder of most of the Jews in Europe. The case is still *sub judice*—but let us hope that the world's conscience may never again slumber while those who believe in right fail to stand up to be counted.

Pope John XXIII (1958–63) will always be known for his gentleness, his understanding, his all-embracing charity. He convoked the Second Vatican Council in 1962, to be the beginning of an *aggiornamento* or "up-dating" or "renewal" of the Roman Catholic Church. To it he invited representatives of the "separated brethren," Orthodox, Anglicans, Protestants, and Liberals, who were given full privileges of attendance as "observers" at all sessions of the Council and access to its official publications, even the proposed decrees (*schemata*) which were still under debate and therefore still *sub secreto*. Nothing like this had happened in five hundred years, and more, of separation and mistrust. No pope ever did so much to win the interest, approval, and even the affection of the *fratres separati,* or to convey to them an understanding of the inner workings of the Roman Catholic Church, or its fundamental convictions, aims, devotion, and purposes. His two immensely influential encyclicals, *Mater et Magistra* (1961; Bettenson 394ff), which summarized the development from Leo's *Rerum novarum* to Pius XI's *Quadragesimo anno* and then on to the present time, and stood directly in this line of advance, and the *Pacem in terris* (1963), his farewell message to all mankind—these will be remembered and studied for generations to come.

When John died on June 3, 1963 the whole world mourned his death, and multitudes wondered where and how a successor of equal stature could be found. The election of Cardinal Montini, Archbishop of Milan, Pope Paul VI, was a fortunate choice. He soon demonstrated his ability and his determination to continue the noble succession of his predecessors, beginning with Leo XIII and culminating in John XXIII. The Vatican Council was continued; its aims remained the same as those appointed it by Pope John. Paul VI entered upon his sacred office with the prayers of all Christendom and the good wishes of all mankind. For the greatest spiritual power in the world was now moving into action, "like a giant awaking from slumber, and preparing to run his course"; like a mighty army, abandoning its century-old strategy of defense and about to launch a strong offensive, and attack the moral and social problems that confront the whole world and threaten not only its peace but its continued existence as a civilized and decent human species.

F. C. G.

BIBLIOGRAPHY

HISTORY

Adamov, E. A. *Die Diplomatie des Vatikans zur Zeit des Imperialismus* (German tr.), Berlin 1932.

Biggs, Anselm G. Art. "Catholic Church," § 3, History: "Growth in the United States," in *Encyclopedia Americana,* VI, 74–77. See also § 4, "Education," and § 5, "Missions."

Cambridge Modern History, 14 vols. Cambridge University Press, 1902–12. New edition in progress.

Caspar, E. *Geschichte des Papsttums,* 2 vols. Tübingen 1930–33.

Corrigan, Raymond. *The Church and the Nineteenth Century.* Milwaukee 1938.

Döllinger, I. von. *La Papauté: son origine au moyen âge et son développement jusqu'en 1870.* (French tr.), Paris 1904, of *Das Papsttum,* Munich 1892.

Ellis, John Tracy. *American Catholicism.* Chicago 1956.

Greenslade, S. L., ed. *The Cambridge History of the Bible: II. The West from the Reformation to the Present Day.* Cambridge Univ. Press 1963. See ch. VI, "The Bible in the Roman Catholic Church from Trent to the Present Day," by F. J. Creehan, S.J.

Guilday, Peter K. *A History of the Councils of Baltimore, 1791–1884.* New York 1932.

Heussi, Karl. *Kompendium der Kirchengeschichte,* 12th ed. Tübingen 1960.

Hoensbroech, P. von. *Das Papsttum in seiner sozialkulturellen Wirksamkeit,* 5th ed. Leipzig 1905–07.

Jalland, T. G. *The Church and the Papacy.* New York 1944.

Lietzmann, Hans. *Petrus und Paulus in Rome,* 3d ed. Berlin 1955.

Loewenich, W. von. *Der Moderne Katholizismus.* Wittenberg 1955.

Mathew, David. *Catholicism in England, 1535–1935,* 3d ed. New York 1936.

Matt, Leonard von, and Hans Kühner. *The Popes* (ill.). Zürich and New York 1963.

Maynard, Theodore. *The Story of American Catholicism.* New York 1941.

Nielson, Fredrik. *The History of the Papacy in the Nineteenth Century,* tr. by A. J. Mason, 2 vols. New York 1906.

Nippold, Friedrich. *The Papacy in the Nineteenth Century,* tr. by L. H. Schwab. New York 1900.

Pastor, Ludwig von. *Geschichte der Päpste seit dem Ausgang des Mittelalters* (to 1800), 16 vols. Eng. tr., London 1891–1953. Vols. XXXIX and XL (tr. by E. F. Perler) contain account of Pius VI (d. 1799).

Putz, Louis J. *The Catholic Church, U.S.A.* Chicago 1956.

Ranke, Leopold von. *Die römischen Päpste in den letzten Vier Jahrhunderten.* 1834–36. New ed. by W. Andreas, Berlin 1957.

Roemer, Theodore. *The Catholic Church in the United States.* St Louis 1950.

Schmidlin, J. *Päpstgeschichte der neuesten Zeit,* 4 vols. Munich 1933–39.

Vollmar, Edw. R. *The Catholic Church in America: a Historical Bibliography.* New Brunswick, New Jersey 1956.

For the most recent history, see also:

Attwater, David. *A Dictionary of the Popes from Peter to Pius XII.* London 1939.

Clancy, John G. *Apostle for our Time: Pope Paul VI.* New York 1963.

Farrow, John. *Pageant of the Popes.* New York 1956.

Hermelink, H. *Die katholische Kirche unter dem Pius-Päpsten des 20. Jahrhunderts.* Zollikon 1949.
Lazzarini, Andreas. *Pope John XXIII.* New York 1959.
Pecher, E. *Pope John XXIII: A Pictorial Biography.* London 1959.
Sugrue, Francis. *Popes in the Modern World.* New York 1961.
See also below, under Vatican II.

VATICAN I

Aubert, R. *Le concile et les conciles.* Paris 1960.
Campana, E. *Il Concilio Vaticano.* Rome 1926.
Butler, Cuthbert. *The Vatican Council 1869–70.* London 1930; paperback edition 1962.
Dejaifve, G. *Pape et évêques au premier Concile du Vatican.* Brügge 1961.
Döllinger, I. von. *Römische Briefe* (by "Quirinus"). Munich 1870.
Friedrich, J. *Geschichte des vatikanischen Konzils,* 3 vols. Bonn 1877–87.
Gibbons, J. (Card.) *Retrospect of Fifty Years.* Baltimore 1917.
Granderath, Th. *Geschichte des vatikanischen Konzils,* 3 vols. St Louis 1903–06.
Hörmann, W. von. *Zur Würdigung des vatikanischen Kirchenrechts.* Innsbruck 1917.
Mourret, F. *Le Concile du Vatican.* Paris 1919.
Rondet, H. *Vatican I: Du Concile de Pie IX au Concile de Jean XXIII.* Paris 1962.
Veuillot, L. *Rome pendant le concile,* 2 vols. Paris 1872.

VATICAN II

Constitution on the Sacred Liturgy: see *Documents,* below.
Daniel-Rops. *Vatican II: Le Concile de Jean XXIII.* Paris 1961. English tr., *The Second Vatican Council.* New York 1962.

Häring, Bernard. *The Johannine Council: Witness to Unity*. New York 1963.

Küng, Hans. *The Council and Reunion;* tr. by Cecily Hastings. New York 1961.

———. *The Council in Action: Theological Reflections on the Second Vatican Council;* tr. by Cecily Hastings. New York 1963.

Lee, Anthony D., ed. *Vatican II: The Theological Dimension*. Washington, D.C. 1963.

Pawley, Bernard. *Looking at the Vatican Council*. London 1962. American edition: *An Anglican View of the Vatican Council*. New York 1962.

"Presbyter Anglicanus." *The Second Vatican Council: An Interim Report*. New York 1963.

"Rynne, Xavier." *Letters from Vatican City. Vatican Council II (First Session): Background and Debates.* New York 1963.

Spina, Tony. *The Pope and the Council* (ill.). New York 1963.

THE CHURCH AND MODERN PROBLEMS

Adam, Karl. *The Spirit of Catholicism*. New York 1929.

———. *One and Holy*. New York 1951.

Biemer, G. *Überlieferung und Offenbarung: die Lehre von der Tradition nach J. H. Newman*. Freiburg 1960.

Bosworth, W. *Catholicism and Crisis in Modern France.* Princeton 1962.

Brantl, Geo. E. *Catholicism*. New York 1961.

Burghardt, W. J., and Lynch, W. F. *The Idea of Catholicism*. New York 1960.

Carrillo de Albornoz, A. F. *Le Catholicisme et la liberté religieuse*. Paris 1961.

Congar, M. J. *La Tradition et les traditions*. Paris 1960.

Corbishley, Thos. *Roman Catholicism*. London 1950. New ed. (paperback) New York 1964.

Eckhardt, Carl C. *The Papacy and World Affairs as Reflected in the Secularization of Politics*. Chicago 1937.

Fülop-Miller, René. *Leo XIII and our Times: the Might of the Church in the World.* Tr. by Conrad Bonacina. New York 1937.

Hartmann, Albert. *Toleranz und Christlicher Glaube.* Frankfort a.M. 1955.

Jalland, T. G. *The Church and the Papacy.* New York 1944.

Klein, Joseph. *Skandalon um das Wesen des Katholizismus.* Tübingen 1958.

Labourdette, M. M. *Foi catholique et problèmes modernes.* Paris 1953.

Lavaud, M.-B. *Sectes modernes et Foi Catholique.* Paris 1954.

Loewenich, W. von. *Modern Catholicism.* New York 1959.

Mackey, Jas. P. *The Modern Theology of Tradition.* London 1962.

Massi, P. *Magistèro infallibile del Papa.* Rome 1957.

Mehl, R. *Du catholicisme romain: approche et interprétation.* Paris 1958.

Micklem, Nathanael. *National Socialism and the Roman Catholic Church.* London 1939.

D'Ormesson, W. *The Papacy.* Tr. by M. Derrick. New York 1959.

Pelikan, Jaroslav. *The Riddle of Roman Catholicism.* New York 1959.

Rahner, Karl. *The Episcopate and the Primacy.* Freiburg, 1962. (French title, 1959: *Dangers dans le Catholicisme d'aujourd'hui.*)

Salmon, George. *The Infallibility of the Church.* New York 1914; abr. ed. 1952.

Scharp, H. *How the Catholic Church is Governed.* Freiburg 1960.

Schellhorn, M. *Der heilige Petrus und seine Nachfolger.* Berlin 1958.

da Veiga Coutinho, L. *Tradition et Histoire dans le controverse moderniste (1898–1910).* Rome 1954.

Winter, Michael. *St Peter and the Popes.* Baltimore 1960.

REUNION

Afanassieff, N., et al. *La primauté de Pierre dans l'Église Orthodoxe.* Neuchâtel and Paris 1960; English tr. 1963.

Baum, Gregory. *That They May be One.* Westminster, Md. 1958.

———. *Progress and Perspectives.* New York 1962.

Bea, Augustine Cardinal. *The Unity of Christians.* New York 1963. English title: *The Catholic Church and the Unity of Christians,* ed. by B. Leeming; London 1963.

See the bibliography in Ch. IX.

——— et al. *L'Église en dialogue.* Paris 1962.

———. *The Ecumenical Council and the Laity.* New York 1961.

Bosc, Jean, Jean Guitton, and Jean Daniélou. *The Protestant-Catholic Dialogue.* Baltimore 1960.

Cavert, Samuel M. *On the Road to Unity.* New York 1961.

Chavaz, E. *Catholicisme romain et protestantisme.* Tournai 1958.

Christiani, L., and P. Rilliet. *Catholiques, Protestants: Les pierres d'achoppement.* 1955. Eng. tr., *Catholics and Protestants: Separated Brothers.* Westminster, Md. 1960.

Cleve, W. T. *Evangelisch und Katholisch,* 5th ed. Wittenberg 1962.

Cullmann, Oscar, et al. *Einheit in Christus: Evangelische und Katholische Bekenntnisse.* Zürich 1960.

———. *Message of Catholics and Protestants.* Grand Rapids 1959.

Esposito, R. F. *Leone XIII e l'Orient Cristiano.* Rome 1961.

Goodall, Norman. *The Ecumenical Movement.* Oxford 1961.

Gordillo, M. *Teologia orientalium cum latinorum comparata.* Rome 1960.

Heenan, John, ed. *Christian Unity: A Catholic View.* London 1962.

Jaeger, Lorenz. *The Ecumenical Council, the Church, and Christendom.* London 1961.

Küng, Hans. *Rechtfertigung: Die Lehre Karl Barths und eine katholische Besinnung,* 3d ed. Paderborn 1960.

de Mendieta, Armand E. *Rome and Canterbury.* London 1962.

Minear, Paul, ed. *The Nature of the Unity we Seek.* St Louis 1958.

Persson, P. E. *Evangelisch und römisch-katholisch.* Göttingen 1961.

Sherrard, P. *The Greek East and the Latin West.* Oxford and New York 1959.

Tavard, G. H. *Protestantism.* New York 1959.

———. *Two Centuries of Ecumenism: The Search for Unity.* Notre Dame 1960; New York (paperback) 1962.

Weigel, Gustave. *Where do we Differ?* London 1962.

DOCUMENTS

Acta Apostolicae Sedis. Rome, since 1909.

Acta Conciliorum Oecumenicorum, ed. by E. Schwartz. Strassburg, 1914 ff.

Acta Sanctae Sedis, 41 volumes. Rome 1865–1908.

Bell, G. K. A. *Documents on Christian Unity, 1920–57.* Oxford 1958.

Bettenson, Henry. *Documents of the Christian Church,* 2d ed. London and New York 1963.

Codex Iuris Canonici. Rome 1918.

Constitution on the Sacred Liturgy, Second Vatican Council, December 4th 1963. Collegeville, Minnesota, 1963.

Denzinger, Henry. *Enchiridion Symbolorum,* 32d edition. New York 1963.

Ellis, John Tracy, ed. *Documents of American Catholic History.* Milwaukee 1956.

———. *Select Bibliography of the History of the Catholic Church in the United States.* New York 1947.

Friedberg, E. *Sammlung der Aktenstücke zum ersten Vatikanischen Concil, mit Grundriss der Geschichte.* Tübingen 1872. Latin text, Nördlingen 1871 ff.

Granderath, Th. *Constitutiones dogmaticae ss. Oecumenici Concilii Vaticani.* Freiburg im Br. 1892.

Guilday, Peter, ed. *The National Pastorals of the American Hierarchy, 1792–1919.* Westminster, Md. 1923.

Hermelink, H., P. Cattin, and H. Th. Conus. *Dokumente von Pius IX bis Pius XII: Heilslehre der Kirche.* Tübingen 1953.

MacGregor, G. *The Vatican Revolution* (documents of Vatican I). Boston 1957.

Mansi, J. D. *Sacrorum Conciliorum Nova et Amplissima Collectio,* 31 vols. Florence 1759–98; still in progress.

Marmy, E. *Mensch und Gemeinschaft in Christlichen Schau: Päpstliche Lehrschriften.* Freiburg in Switzerland 1945.

Mirbt, Carl. *Quellen zur Geschichte des Papsttums und des Römischen Katholizismus,* 4th ed. Tübingen 1924.

Pius XII: Documents Pontificaux 1948–58, 11 vols. Rome 1944 ff.

Powers, Francis J., ed. *Papal Pronouncements on the Political Order.* Westminster, Md., 1952.

Treacy, Gerald C., ed. *Five Great Encyclicals.* New York 1939.

Wilson, George, ed. *Truth, Unity, Peace:* Encyclical of Pope John XXIII. New York 1959. *See also:*

Gibbons, Wm. J., tr. *Mater et Magistra,* by Pope John XXIII ("Christianity and Social Progress"). New York 1962.

Pacem in Terris. Last Encyclical of Pope John XXIII. Rome 1963.

REFERENCE WORKS

Annuario Pontificio. Rome (annual).

A Catholic Dictionary of Theology, ed. by H. F. Davis et al. Vol. I, New York 1962.

Catholic Directory. London (annual).

Catholic Encyclopaedia, 15 volumes and Index. New York 1907–14. New edition in preparation.

Dictionnaire de Droit Canonique, ed. by R. Naz et al. Paris 1924.

Enciclopedia Cattolica, ed. by P. Paschini et al., 12 volumes. Rome 1949–54.

Lexikon für Theologie und Kirche, ed. by M. Buchberger, 10 vols. Freiburg im Br., 1930–38. New ed. by J. Höfer and K. Rahner, 1957 ff.

The Oxford Dictionary of the Christian Church, ed. by F. L. Cross. London and New York, 1957.

Realencyklopädie für Protestantische Theologie und Kirche, ed. by J. J. Herzog and A. Hauck, 22 vols. Leipzig 1898–1909; *Supplement,* 2 vols., 1913.

Religion in Geschichte und Gegenwart, 2d ed., 5 vols. and *Index,* Tübingen 1927–31. 3d ed., 6 vols., 1957–62; *Index* to follow.

Twentieth Century Encyclopaedia of Religious Knowledge (extension of the *New Schaff-Herzog Encyclopaedia of Religious Knowledge*), ed. by L. A. Loetscher. Grand Rapids, 2 vols. 1955.

INDEX